VESTIGES OF GRANDEUR

VESTIGES OF GRANDEUR

THE PLANTATIONS OF LOUISIANA'S RIVER ROAD

TEXT AND PHOTOGRAPHS BY Richard Sexton

AERIAL PHOTOGRAPHS BY Alex S. MacLean

INTRODUCTION BY Eugene Cizek

CHRONICLE BOOKS

SAN FRANCISCO

Library of Congress Cataloging-in-Publication Data:
Sexton, Richard.
    Vestiges of grandeur: the plantations of Louisiana's River Road / by Richard Sexton;
introduction by Eugene Cizek; aerial photographs by Alex MacLean.
    p. cm.
    Includes bibliographical references and index.
ISBN 0-8118-1817-9
    1. Plantations—Louisiana—River Road. 2. Architecture, Modern—17th–18th centuries—
Louisiana—River Road. 3. Architecture, Modern—19th century—Louisiana—River Road.
I. Maclean, Alex S. II. Title.
NA7613.L8S48   1999   99-127478
728' .09763'3—dc21   CIP

Printed in Hong Kong

FACING TITLE PAGE: Row of slave cabins at Evergreen Plantation
FACING TABLE OF CONTENTS: Attic stair leading to the belvedere at Evergreen Plantation.

DESIGNED BY Charles Routhier and Joseph Jurewicz/Storehouse Co.

Distributed in Canada by Raincoast Books
8680 Cambie Street
Vancouver, British Columbia V6P 6M9

10 9 8 7 6 5 4 3 2

Chronicle Books
85 Second Street
San Francisco, California 94105

www.chroniclebooks.com

DEDICATION

Dedicated to all those individuals across time whom fate has dealt the most vexing of destinies—
THE PURSUIT OF LOST CAUSES.

A baby portrait of Noémie Jones, known by her family as Tante Dubonne, who in 1894 was born the daughter of
Adam Barthelemy Jones, a River Road cane planter like his father before him. Noémie lived the entirety of her life
in the family's plantation house in Edgard, Louisiana, enjoying the good times and weathering the bad on land her
family has always owned. In 1965, Hurricane Betsy blew the roof off the old house, yet she and her sister Imelda
persevered, bailing rainwater out of the place, with the help of relatives, for days afterward. She died on February
14, 1982, at the age of eighty-eight. This portrait hangs in what had been the dining room of the plantation house,
which is now empty and unoccupied.

CONTENTS

PREFACE

BETWEEN NEW ORLEANS AND BATON ROUGE, ALONG what has become very much a minor route, lies a low landscape haunted in a poetic way both by the historical myth of the Old South and by the contemporary trappings of a petrochemical empire. This meandering corridor is referred to locally as the River Road, a singularity that is something of a misnomer for the serpentine, narrow highways tracing both banks of the river at the levee's base. Between rows of sugarcane reaching a vanishing point at a swampy infinity, industrial apparitions loom large— oil refineries, petrochemical plants, power plants, and a host of other mysterious structures. Antebellum plantation architecture is sprinkled randomly along the Road, interspersed with low-slung ranch houses and mobile homes. These sit amid mowed yards and a variety of solid remnants, such as chimneys, that are the only remains of the more substantial architecture and the more lucrative livelihood that once existed here. The architectural declension of the River Road is rather sobering, since it points inevitably to the increasingly meager way of life on this land.

The River Road today is not an environment of compelling harmony. Nonetheless, here and there, the adventurous explorer will readily uncover the most incredible things. Exploring the River Road is a powerful, unique experience, but this fact may be lost on the casual observer due to what might be termed "fragmentation." What was once a rich agrarian culture has been supplanted by a modern industrial culture of equal economic consequence that has fostered a very different kind of architecture. The contemporary River Road is a random mosaic of historic fragments separated by completely unrelated stuff. My particular intrigue is not to be judgmental of the River Road's complex history and present, but to bear witness to the baroque spectacle of mankind's exploitation of a

River Road cane fields at St. John the Baptist Parish line.

fertile landscape. A swampy wilderness became a compelling place of human habitation and entrepreneurship that, in about a century's time, was completely transformed. Through it all, some evocative vestiges of this ancient past have survived to haunt the present. They are the subject, and namesake, of this book.

It may seem rather presumptuous to consider a past this recent as ancient, but when measured by that episodic perspective, which judges time more by the extent of dramatic change than so many movements of a clock's hands, this culture and the feudal society it fostered are indeed ancient. In fact, they were ancient even when they were new.

The most conspicuous vestiges along the River Road are the great plantation houses that gaze apprehensively toward a massive levee; but as majestic as these houses are, they are only the most dominant component of a more complex plantation culture. Overseer's houses, slave cabins, and an array of farm buildings and outbuildings were the supporting components of the plantation sites. Churches and cemeteries,

steamboat landings, plantation stores, and occasional small towns contributed to the agrarian settlement pattern. Here and there, vestiges of all these elements linger along the River Road, forming a complex melange.

From a historical perspective, to focus exclusively on the River Road between New Orleans and Baton Rouge is to offer only a partial view of a much bigger story. Waterways, tributaries, and distributaries of the great Mississippi River covered all of south Louisiana, and many very significant plantations, such as Madewood and Parlange, both of which have survived to the present, are not located on the River Road. In a contemporary sense, however, the River Road is a defined region—a corridor of commerce and development. This topical condition helps establish meaningful parameters for a subject that, if not adequately defined, would be too much for the pages of any one book to contain. The historical architecture of the River Road, from New Orleans to Baton Rouge, thus became my exclusive focus. The boundaries are the Orleans Parish line downriver and the old Baton

The Speak Easy Bar in Vacherie, Louisiana.

Rouge bridge upriver. Only those plantations with River frontage, or back parcel plantations that relied on the river for market access, are included.

Even within these geographic constraints, an important component of this ancient feudal society—the city of New Orleans, the vital trading post where the planter's crops were brought to market—is not covered within these pages. New Orleans became much more than just a center of trade. It was where an urban society and culture could be found, where crops were financed, and where vital goods and supplies could be procured. It was in New Orleans that planters kept townhouses to live in during the winter and stay in during frequent business trips to the city. While New Orleans is very much a vestige of the plantation culture of south Louisiana, I did not include it for the personal reason that it had been the subject of one of my previous books, *New Orleans:*

Elegance and Decadence. Though *Elegance and Decadence* was not intended to expressly depict New Orleans as the planters would have known it, it is about the historical architecture and neighborhoods of the city and what they are like today. I would characterize *Vestiges of Grandeur* as a continuation of the process of photographic exploration that *Elegance and Decadence* began. In a sense, the two have become volumes of the same related story.

Though the geographic parameters of my subject are rigidly defined, it is impossible to include all the region's historic architecture; nevertheless, I strove for *Vestiges* to be representative. Because of Louisiana's beginnings as a French agrarian colony, it is unique within the Southern experience. It was in south Louisiana that Creole, Anglo, and African traditions blended to create a distinctive New World culture. The River Road thus is not merely a random slice of the antebellum South, but a rare subculture embedded within it. In the choice of buildings that could be included here, the dominant criterion was a good, representative mix—age, size, condition, type, and style were all considered in determining what should be included.

The photographic essay presented here comprises four broad themes: the pattern of settlement, the realm of the interior, the ambience of the countryside, and the cultural landscape. The opening chapter, "The Pattern of Settlement," is an orientation setting the stage for the more detailed explorations that follow. It shows the general makeup of the River Road, the types of buildings found on plantation sites, the towns and communities, and the major principal houses. Most of the plantation houses are shown in greater detail in subsequent chapters, but the general information of date, builder, location, type, and style is given in chapter one. "The Realm of the Interior" is an intimate look into the private world behind the colonnades and French doors of the plantation residences. Some of the houses included are open to the public, but most are not. This chapter thus explores a world that the average person never gets to see. "The Ambience of the Countryside" explores the natural rural setting that characterizes life on the River Road. It includes not just gardens and *allées* framing the principal houses, but aspects of agriculture from the cane harvest to raising livestock. "The Cultural Landscape," the culmination of the photo essay and the most abstract part of it, focuses on the culture that underlies life on the River Road—the values, pursuits, religions, and rituals of the people who make their home and livelihood here. The intent of this thematic approach is to offer a holistic view of the subject rather than a series of "spreads" of chosen houses. Typically, this thematic approach assigns an archetypal context to the subject and portrays it not just for what it is, but for how it defines an architectural or functional type, the char-

acter of a pattern, or the ideal of a people. This book can be experienced in many ways, but it is intended that it be "read" from front to back.

There is a deliberate tension in my thematic approach to this work that characterizes my work generally. It is the tension between the artist and the journalist within me. I take great pains to glorify and immortalize my subject as only an artist would do, but my greater interest is to articulate and evangelize a cause as only a journalist would do. There is a simple answer to the probable conceptual debate as to whether this work is an artistic interpretation of the River Road or a journalistic documentation of it: It is both of these things.

A distinguishing characteristic that gradually emerged among the historic buildings I photographed has to do with condition, but it cannot be described

Abandoned grocery store in Convent, Louisiana.

Words of encouragement for River Road travelers in St. John the Baptist Parish.

exclusively by that alone. The uncertain future that many houses and buildings now face is a related aspect. I particularly find those plantation buildings mired in a state of partial or total ruin to be the most compelling subjects. Ruins are architecture stripped bare, revealed in a way that it could never be otherwise. The predicament of ruin evokes tragedy in a particularly haunting way. Like the nude, architectural ruins can possess a disturbing vulnerability. The notion that a transitory condition has been permanently etched on film is inherent. The photographing of ruins is thus a form of catharsis, mitigating a condition pregnant with uncertainty, doubt, and melancholy.

For a number of years, I somehow managed to avoid the River Road altogether. I was not prepared for the subject, what it symbolized historically, and the contemporary conditions that threatened to undermine it, or for the powerful gestalt left by those artists and writers who had interpreted it before me. At least subliminally, I knew that this place would be a point of intense focus one day. After about five years of residency in New Orleans, that time finally arrived, albeit haphazardly. A friend took me to see his family's ancestral house in Edgard, on the west bank. Actually, the point of the trip was to explore the swamps around Lake Des Allemands, which I had expressed an interest in seeing; but the old family house on River Road made the stronger impression. As impressed as I was with the old house, however, I was not prepared for its broader context. It recalled in the most dramatic of ways a personal experience of over twenty years ago.

In the late summer of 1976, I arrived in Athens, Greece, after an enervating overnight flight from New York. The true beginning of the trip, in my mind, was to have been Istanbul, not Athens; but the Greeks and Turks were threatening renewed conflict in their perpetual war, and I couldn't get a train immediately. So with time on my hands, I did what most every other tourist of modern-day Athens has done and ascended the Acropolis to gaze upon the ruins of the Parthenon. Though I certainly didn't realize it then, over time I came to acknowledge that at the Acropolis I had witnessed the ultimate fate of all architecture. Few buildings, in fact, leave as significant a ruin as a Greek temple. Most architecture ultimately requires an archeological dig and an array of artists' conceptual drawings to show us what once was.

Reflecting on my visit to the Parthenon, I remember most the whiteness of the stone. Earlier that same year I had seen Nashville, Tennessee's full-scale reproduction of the Parthenon, which was made of exposed aggregate (or some similar historically incorrect brown material). My second most memorable impression of the Parthenon—the genuine, Athenian one—was its context. Young backpacking tourists posed for snapshots on ancient rubble embellished with the carved initials and graffitti of previous, even less-restrained visitors. Nearby, sodas and postcards were purveyed from small wheeled carts. The auspicious icon that had come to symbolize the emergence of Western civilization was, above all else, a tourist destination. Whatever my expectations might have been for the Parthenon, I was not adequately prepared for this. The replicant Nashville Parthenon was, at least, set amid a pristinely landscaped municipal park—a more reverential context, certainly.

The context of the plantations on Louisiana's River Road was about as unexpected as the Parthenon's had been. Mythological places, like myths, become painfully debunked when subjected to the merciless ravages of overzealously objective scrutiny. My predominant focus in this work is the poetic vestiges of plantation life, which enjoy the great good fortune of having survived to the present. On the other hand, as a journalist I can neither follow the rut of the Southern mythologists who have chronicled plantation culture as a grand Arcadian utopia, nor skirt entirely the contemporary conditions that threaten these surviving vestiges I so treasure. Context can be just as relevant and significant as it is a distraction. The telling of this story with all the pathos inherent in it is a matter of precarious balance. This is a Gothic tale encumbered by a Gothic form of beauty both compelling and repulsive, tragic and romantic all at the same time. It engenders a nostalgic desire for a past no one can go back to and a hope for a future that must be envisioned through a veil of impenetrable complexity.

RICHARD SEXTON

INTRODUCTION

THE MISSISSIPPI RIVER BEGINS IN THE STREAMS AND lakes of Canada and the midwestern United States, which form major rivers that merge to create one of the most powerful river systems in the world. The basin that is created by this vast flow of water is larger than that of China's Yellow River, twice the size of Africa's Nile and India's Ganges. It includes the majority of the continental United States and two Canadian provinces. The valley of the river, which includes the drainage area of its major tributary, the Missouri, is like a giant funnel that gathers water from Montana to New York and twists and turns its way to the Gulf of Mexico, interconnecting the heartland of North America over its 3,740-mile length. A complex natural and built environment has evolved along this transportational and cultural lifeline. The land at the lower end of the valley, in what is now Louisiana, was the least stable; the Mississippi migrated from one new river bed to another at least seven times. These changes created new deltas as old land disappeared into the Gulf of Mexico. The ecological system that evolved is one of the most complex and sensitive in the world today.

This is the framework for the magic land of old Louisiana, particularly the winding strip of riverfront running from New Orleans to Baton Rouge. The early French and Spanish settlers, drawing on building concepts of the indigenous Native American population that made living in the heat and humidity of the region as comfortable as possible, established housing patterns that, by the early nineteenth century, evolved into plantation architecture. Through periods of growth and decline, war and reconstruction, devastating floods and pounding hurricanes, industrial challenge and contemporary indifference, the ancient houses, exotic landscape, and hypnotic legends of the River Road have continued to captivate resident and visitor alike.

The first European to see the mouth of the Mississippi was Spanish explorer Hernando de Soto, who encountered it on his travels through the Gulf of Mexico en route to Mexico in 1542. Nearly 150 years later, in 1682, Robert Cavalier de La Salle traveled the Great Lakes from Canada and descended the river to the Gulf of Mexico. He claimed all of the lands drained by this vast water system in the name of King Louis XIV of France and called the new colonial territory "Louisiane" in honor of the king. In 1685, La Salle returned to the Gulf of Mexico to establish a new settlement for France, but he was unable to find the river's mouth, landing instead in what is now Texas.

The French Canadian explorer Pierre le Moyne d'Iberville successfully found the mouth of the river in 1699 and reclaimed the territory for France. In the same year, his brother, Jean Baptiste le Moyne de Bienville, persuaded a party of English explorers to abandon its quest to claim the river region for England, and sealed the fate of Louisiana to become a French colony.

The primary purpose of colonization was to create wealth and power for the mother country, since competition for New World resources was fierce. Louisiana and its vast territory slowly became important as a site for colonization. The Mississippi River became an immense conduit for the transportation of goods, services, and influence, and the higher ground of the natural levees provided locations for a built environment, offering protection from flooding and respite from the lushness and overabundance of nature.

After several false starts at colonial development in the early 1700s, the Company of the Indies was formed in 1717, with Scots-born entrepreneur John Law as its director. Law was given a twenty-year charter with the understanding that he would increase the population of Louisiana to 10,000 within a ten-year period, adding about 6,000 free people and 3,000 slaves to the meager extant population of 400.

The first five years of Law's control saw the colony of Louisiana expand rapidly. Wealthy French citizens were granted large concessions of land. African slaves, chosen for their skill in farming and construction and acquired primarily from Senegal and Gambia, were imported to develop an agricultural base. Thousands of German farmers were also encouraged to immigrate and were given small concessions of land. They settled along the river above New Orleans and created the German Coast, which, by 1746, had become the second-largest area of population. The industrious farmers prospered and enjoyed a reputation as the "bread basket" of the new colony. With their German names changed to French, many of the families became large landowners along the river or rich entrepreneurs in New Orleans.

New Orleans was founded in 1718 by Bienville and was named in honor of the Duc d'Orleans. Four years later, as the Mississippi River gained importance, the capital of the Louisiana colony was transferred to New Orleans from Mobile. Life began slowly in the young city, following the prescribed organization of land and architecture as set forth by the Royal Engineers. A rectilinear pattern of three-hundred-foot squares was arranged around a plaza where public buildings—both church and government—faced the river. The more important buildings were generally placed parallel to the river to enjoy the prevailing winds. The architecture followed the precepts long established in colonies such as Saint Domingue, now Haiti, in the Caribbean.

The Royal Engineers also established settlement patterns upriver from New Orleans. In order to maximize access to the primary watery corridors, land for development was arranged in long, narrow concessions perpendicular to the river. The French arpent, approximately 192 linear feet, became the unit measure; a square arpent equaled about five-sixths of an acre. Land was granted along the river frontage with

Along the river, the old imprints of French colonial land grants are readily visible today. The long wedge-shaped parcels maximized vital river frontage for the planters.

depths of either forty or eighty arpents, creating long, pie-shaped parcels.

When the Europeans arrived in Louisiana, they found an exotic world of subtropical landscape and indigenous culture. The Native Americans were highly skilled at creating architecture for their hot, humid climate. They understood how comfort could be derived through the use of pavilions and galleries that allowed airflow to permeate the interiors and covered areas of their structures. They used a building technique that incorporated large poles placed in the ground for strength and smaller interwoven tree branches to create wall and roof surfaces. This structure was then covered with a composition of mud, moss, and animal hair; burned oyster shell was added if a solid surface was desired, while palmetto fronds were utilized if a more airy space was needed. Large sections of tree bark were used for more complex structures. Wall surfaces were decorated with cultural images and adorned with projections of other materials to indicate a structure's use and status. Galleries were added to provide shade and to protect the openings from rain. Trelliage, an open framework of vertical

and horizontal construction, in time would become covered in vines to totally integrate nature with the man-made.

Midway between Baton Rouge and New Orleans, on a great vacherie, a grassy plain of high ground, the French found the amazing city of the Colapissa Indians, called Tabiscania. To escape floodwaters and catch the prevailing breezes, the native people had built their structures along the narrow breech of high ground on the natural levee. This linear development stretched for almost seven miles and housed more than a thousand inhabitants. Tabiscania was not a primitive site but a well-planned community totally integrated with nature, and it served as a model for many of the French villages and plantations that developed during the early days of colonization.

This wonderful native architecture was described by French explorers and drawn by artists in their journals, giving us the few images we have today. These same artists also drew the early French importations of architecture, creating naive but richly detailed Louisiana images. One such example, from Chouachas, a land grant made some twenty-one miles below New

The relationship between the principal house at Evergreen Plantation and its primary outbuildings is revealed in this aerial view. To the sides of the principal house are the pigeonniers and garçonnières with a parterre garden uniting a plantation office, kitchen building, and privy behind.

Orleans on the west bank of the Mississippi, is a drawing by French artist Dumont de Montigny that has become a critical document in illustrating the character of rural land settlements along the river. The drawing shows the rectilinear development of fenced yards and gardens on the high-ground levee. Hand-hewn *pieux*, or palisade, fences of cypress were impaled in the ground to protect the main house, and a French-style parterre garden was positioned to the rear of the yard. The houses follow the design of French farms that had evolved from the traditions of Italian engineer-designers like Sebastiano Serlio.

The historian Le Page du Pratz, once manager of the Company of the Indies, wrote in great detail about another site across from New Orleans, near present-day Algiers. Du Pratz described a main house flanked by pigeon houses, or *pigeonniers.* Other support structures, including a kitchen, a chapel, slave lodgings, and animal coops, were located to each side of the main house in neat order. The coops were surrounded by smaller *pieux* fencing. Along the rectilinear street system at the rear were barns and storehouses; farther downriver, in their own square village, were several slave cabins and a support building. This image would be at home in the French countryside if not for the context of verdant south Louisiana plant materials.

French tradition was indeed the dominant cultural force in Louisiana during the period. Despite the Native American, African, Spanish, and German presence, the French would prevail as the initial ingredient of Creole culture, establishing a strong presence that tempers the region even today. The word *creole* in French descends from the Spanish word *criollo,* which comes from the Latin verb *creare,* meaning "to create in a new place." First-born children in the New World would be known as Creoles, a label that was also extended to slave children. The architecture that evolved and that responded to the demands of climate and available materials was similarly classified, as were plant materials, customs, speech patterns, and culture.

In 1734, French engineer Bernard de Verges prepared the first documented design for a structure that incorporated the features necessary for a building to survive and create comfort in the hot, humid environment of south Louisiana. The design for a guardhouse to be

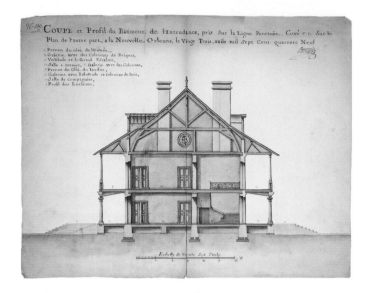

An architectural section for Ignace Broutin's Intendance Building, an administrative building in New Orleans that was never built. It is the earliest known plan for a building that incorporates the galleries and broken-pitch roof that would come to define Creole plantation principal houses. (Photograph courtesy Barbara SoRelle Bacot.)

erected at the Balise, near the mouth of the Mississippi, called for the building to be raised off the ground several feet by continuous and deep foundation walls of brick. A gallery across the front was totally incorporated under a roof structure of mortise and tenon Norman-truss design. This basic form of heavy timber construction was strong and could withstand the intense wind, rain, and hurricanes of Louisiana. De Verges's plan called for rooms opening one into the other without a hall, in the French colonial tradition. Because of the galleries, shutters and casement windows could be opened during a rain without the interior spaces becoming soaked. The emphasis of the plan was on cross ventilation and protection from the elements—Creole architecture was born.

The only remaining intact French colonial building in New Orleans is the Ursuline Convent, on Chartres Street, which was constructed in 1745 from the design of Ignace Francois Broutin, a Royal Engineer. It replaced an earlier design by Broutin that had begun to deteriorate even before its completion.

The earliest architectural designs failed to understand the problems of building on poor soils, and the exposed-timber superstructure in the brick-between-post walls could not withstand the rains of south Louisiana. The changes made in foundation type and basic building materials were integral to the development of Creole architecture.

These French colonial designs established the pattern for plantation architecture that would be utilized throughout Louisiana, especially on the River Road between Baton Rouge and New Orleans. In the early plantation buildings there, the walls were built on a continuous foundation to spread the load into the weak soil. If the first floor was to be used primarily for living space, it typically was elevated and wood was the surfacing material. If the use was to be more for storage and/or support activities, the first floor was usually brick—still elevated, but to a lesser degree.

In these early structures, the wood that was the basis for heating required massive fireplaces, which were decorated with boxed or wraparound mantels.

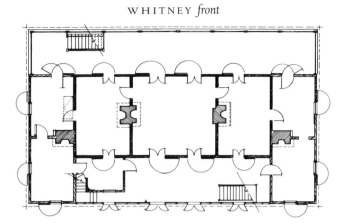

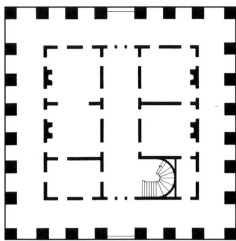

The floor plan of the principal house at Whitney Plantation is a prototypical example of the layout of Creole plantation houses—the lack of interior hallways, cabinet enclosing a rear loggia, and the main living level on the second floor. In contrast, the floor plan of the principal house at Ashland Plantation exemplifies Anglo-American influence, characterized by a grand center hall on both floors. This Georgian-derived plan features a layout of rooms that is essentially identical on both floors with the parlors downstairs and bedrooms upstairs. Later Creole houses came to adopt this floor plan. (Ashland floor plan courtesy Louisiana Division of Historic Preservation; Department of Culture, Recreation & Tourism.)

The decorative details of these chimneypieces were coordinated with other aspects of a room's design. Reception rooms, parlors, and dining rooms had the most elaborate details, and their mantels often included paneled and hand-carved overmantels. Baseboards, door surrounds, and ceiling cornices complemented each other to create a *tout ensemble*, or overall completeness in design. These details were executed in wood and painted, often in faux finishes, to resemble richer, more exotic materials. The finishes would vary depending on the wealth of the owner or the level of wealth the owner wished to imply. The Creoles of this era, however, tended to be less showy of their economic means than the Anglo-Americans who would come to the River Road later.

The early plantations were of two types—either manager-occupied or owner-occupied. Owner-occupied plantations of medium or large size usually also had an overseer who assisted in the direction of labor and kept order and industry when the owner and his family were living in their city house in New Orleans. The primary crops grown on these early plantations were indigo, rice, corn, and tobacco, but these were not enough for sustained growth. In 1751, the Jesuits, who had purchased the plantation Bienville established above New Orleans, introduced a variety of sugarcane that showed promise in Louisiana's subtropical climate. Sugar production had produced vast wealth in French colonies in the Caribbean, and it was seen as a possible salvation for the still-struggling Louisiana. Sugar soon became the dominant cash crop on the River Road, and its importance was strengthened when entrepreneurs in the region developed both a granulation process and a procedure to refine raw sugar.

Throughout the latter half of the eighteenth century, south Louisiana felt the effects of the political and colonial turmoil of both Europe and the New World. As a result of the Seven Years War, in 1762 France transferred control over portions of its territory to both Spain and England. As England destroyed France's Canadian bastion, the Acadian French left Nova Scotia rather than swear allegiance to England, and by 1764 they began to arrive in Louisiana, which had been ceded to Spain. The Acadians related to a rural way of life, and the Cajun culture they founded evolved as the most lasting French-language tradition in Louisiana.

When Spain supported the revolution of the English colonies, Louisiana became a focus of that conflict. Spain ultimately returned the Territory of Louisiana to France in 1800, although just five years earlier the young United States had been granted permanent trade access to the port of New Orleans. The sudden transfer created uneasiness in the United States for fear that Napoleon would close the strategic port to trade, and President Thomas Jefferson sent representatives to France to negotiate the purchase of the Isle of Orleans. In great financial need, Napoleon offered to sell the entire territory for $15 million; Jefferson acted quickly and, in a single transaction that startled the entire world, the United States doubled in size.

In the years prior to Louisiana's admission as the eighteenth state of the Union in 1812, French Creole culture was challenged at every point. In 1808, a new law prohibited the continued importation of slaves; slave revolts followed in some parishes, but the rebels were defeated and the slaves put on trial and executed. While Creoles expressed interest in declaring their own independence as a freestanding republic during this period, they nevertheless played an integral part in the process toward statehood, accepting responsible leadership in the new state. By 1815, when the British met their final defeat on the plantation lands of St. Bernard Parish below New Orleans, the steamboat era on the Mississippi had begun; the interiors of these great moving palaces competed regally with the increasingly sumptuous interiors of the plantation principal houses and city mansions.

The Creoles began to prosper in ways they never had before. Sugar had become an international business, and Louisiana became one of the industry's largest and richest players. Though epidemics of malaria, yellow fever, and cholera, along with hurricanes and floods, wreaked havoc on the population, plantation culture grew richer and richer. The empire, centered along the Mississippi River Road and its tributaries, made New Orleans one of the most powerful cities in the world, and the sugar barons of south Louisiana assumed a stature alongside that of the cotton kings from Northern Louisiana and the other Southern states. This success allowed the plantation settlements to expand on past traditions and evolve into opulent country settings. Their interiors glistened with furniture and decorative arts that rivaled the grandest of the Old and New worlds. Churches, cemeteries, commercial development, and growing urban settings proclaimed to the world that Louisiana was special and important.

As the Creole plantation house and its setting evolved, one facet of the region's new status was manifested in an interest in the Classical Revival styles in architecture; a development made possible by the great wealth of the River Road plantations and fueled by the planters' increasingly frequent European travel. Creoles and Americans alike made the Grand Tour and brought home fine furniture, decorative and fine arts, and the desire to rebuild the public image of their estates. Individual designs created by architects, as well as plans taken from pattern books, gave master builders guidelines for the new styles.

The raised Creole plantation house, with its surrounding galleries, was a natural receptacle for the new ideals of classicism, and the climate-responsive Creole structures assumed the form of Greek or Roman temples. The marriage of Creole vernacular with classical temple forms was also a natural response to the not-forgotten ideal of a Creole republic and empire;

This sequence of HABS elevations of the principal house at Destrehan Plantation reveals the evolution of a Creole building over time. The first elevation shows how the house looked when constructed in 1787. The second elevation shows the addition of side wings added in 1812. The third elevation shows the results of a remodeling in 1840 when the Creole building was altered to conform to the Classical style that had come into vogue. The turned colonettes above the heavy masonry first floor columns of 1787 were replaced with two-story, classically detailed masonry columns.

the myths and realities of the South found a new mode of expression as early Creole plantations were remodeled to reflect the new classical tastes. Two-storied, classically detailed masonry columns replaced the original column alignments of wooden colonettes placed above first-floor masonry columns, and doors and windows were embellished with Greek key trim.

Many towns along the River Road added important Greek Revival and Italianate landmarks. Perhaps the greatest collection was in the town of Convent, where beautiful early Creole cottages blended harmoniously with later classical structures of every size. Sacred Heart Women's College, built in the mid-nineteenth century, was a wonder of Gothic style mixed with other inspirations. Since demolished, Sacred Heart once housed and educated young women from the finest families of Louisiana's plantation society. Nearby was Jefferson College, a school for men chartered in 1831 and supported by the leading plantation owners of the area. After fire destroyed much of the campus in 1842, it was rebuilt in the Classical Revival style. St. Michael's Church nearby was built in the Gothic Revival style in 1833. Convent has lost many historic structures, but it still maintains a special image of the past. Donaldsonville, White Castle, and Plaquemine

also saw the creation of many antebellum landmarks, but only vestiges of this grandeur remain today.

A sense of euphoria continued along the River Road during the mid nineteenth century as a result of this tremendous expansion and wealth, despite the growing threat of war over the issue of slavery. On the eve of the American Civil War, over four hundred major principal houses and their plantation settings sat along a stretch of the Mississippi extending south from Natchez through New Orleans; the majority of the millionaires in the United States lived in this zone of wealth. The Lower Mississippi Valley was one of the world's most unique and important cultures, but the war would bring its downfall and set the context for the period of Reconstruction.

Louisiana seceded from the United States in 1861 and remained an independent nation for two months, when pressures from both the Confederacy and the Union forced its decision to join the Confederacy. Many citizens of Louisiana felt that slavery was morally wrong and/or economically unwise; and many wealthy planters and abolitionists alike publicly voiced these feelings. There was also a strong movement in Louisiana that celebrated the region's uniqueness and its isolation from both the South and the North.

This aerial view of Houmas House illustrates a different form of evolution from Destrehan. In this example, a grand classical villa of about 1840 has been appended to a modest eighteenth-century French colonial structure at the rear. The original house has retained its roof shape and is joined to the newer house by a hyphen structure.

Then, as today, many Louisianians, particularly those from Creole New Orleans and Acadian Lafayette, felt a sense of regionalism bordering on nationalism; the idea of being a port city open to both sides of the conflict represented a time-honored tradition.

Louisiana did not last long as part of the Confederacy. Both sides knew the importance of New Orleans, and its Mississippi River linkage of Canada to the Gulf of Mexico was critical to eventual success; in 1862 the New Orleans region fell to the Union forces. The state capital was quickly moved from Baton Rouge, where the Gothic Revival capitol building was destroyed by fire, to Opelousas and finally to Shreveport, where the overall demise of the Confederacy in Louisiana occurred in 1865. In 1868, the harsh Reconstruction government approved for Louisiana instigated a series of actions that continued to devastate the resources and spirit of the state's population. White and black citizens alike were repressed as individual corrupt fortunes were amassed by a few to the detriment of many.

During the 1870s, the steamboat culture and economy grew to unprecedented heights as land and agricultural development changed hands. Most Louisiana planters were destroyed by the war and were forced to sell their lands for unpaid taxes at fractions of their real value. The scorched-earth policy was selectively enforced, however, with New Orleans being spared; economic development in the Creole capital continued throughout these years. By the time President Rutherford B. Hayes ended Reconstruction and the longest Union Army occupation of any state in 1877, the conquering party had built new personal palaces in the city and acquired thousands of acres of agriculture and related plantation settings.

The last quarter of the nineteenth century saw many advances in the technique and technology of sugarcane farming. In 1884, the World's Industrial and Cotton Centennial Exposition opened in New Orleans on the former site of Etienne de Boré's sugar plantation—now Audubon Park, across St. Charles Avenue from Tulane and Loyola Universities. The exposition was an attempt to reestablish Louisiana and New Orleans as world-class trading and cultural partners. There had been continuous research in the quest for a suitable type of cane that would withstand the subtropical weather, ravenous insects, and evolving diseases of the region—Louisiana State University, founded earlier in the century, played a crucial role in that research—but even this effort could not prevent major agricultural catastrophes. The cumulative effect of the cultural upheaval and the uncertainties of plantation agriculture during the century had led to the demise of the small, individual plantation sugar mill and the creation of larger and larger cooperative operations. Each of these events in its own way changed the patterns of ownership, wealth, and identity along the River Road.

In 1901, oil was discovered in southwestern Louisiana and a new competitor for the great lands along the Mississippi River was born. As the petrochemical industry evolved, the vertical masonry chimneys of the sugar mills changed to a complex landscape of metal pipes and smokestacks that grew as the technology required more and taller vertical structures. Some of the world's richest and most agriculturally productive land was transferred to new and static uses, and the region between Baton Rouge and New Orleans would become the largest petrochemical complex in the world. One by one, planta-

tions would be sold for new uses that typically resulted in a complete demolition of the great architecture and landscape. Europe's Ruhr Valley had been transplanted to Louisiana, and just as the great castles and picturesque villages of the Ruhr had slowly disappeared, yielding to a modern idea of progress, so did the plantation settings of Louisiana.

In the first decades of the twentieth century, as Standard Oil built one of the largest oil refineries in the world in Baton Rouge, other events impacted the culture and land along the River Road. In 1915, one of the most powerful hurricanes in recorded history hit south Louisiana, devastating New Orleans and the great houses and lands of the Sugar Empire. Almost three hundred people lost their lives and thousands were left homeless. The eve of World War I brought both power and destruction to the River Road, as the nation's need for fuel and petrochemical products made Baton Rouge a world leader in production. New Orleans became a major materials supplier and ship builder in the war effort. South Louisiana had been thrust into the new century.

In 1927, floodwaters began to rise in the northern hinterlands of the Mississippi River, creating a force never seen or felt before in the United States. Over one-third of Louisiana was inundated, and close to one million people were forced from their homes. Thousands died. The Red Cross fed almost a million people for months while politicians and entrepreneurs at all levels attempted to cope with the situation. The forces that contributed to the Great Flood of 1927 began in the nineteenth century, when humankind first attempted to control the flow and future of the Mississippi. Before then, of course, the river had flowed freely back and forth over the landscape, creating its rich deltas and their corresponding riverbeds; the flood was symbolic of the opposing ideological and political battles that had been fought at the natural waterway's expense.

The following year, Huey P. Long, from north Louisiana, was elected governor, promising new hope to all of those suffering from the Great Flood as well as to the huge numbers of Louisiana citizens disenfranchised since Reconstruction. Both as governor and later, as U.S. Senator, Long struck economic deals with the petrochemical industry that created personal wealth and power unknown in his time; the consequences of these actions still control much of the River Road. Despite his often-despotic behavior, however, Long did bring the rural Louisiana areas beyond the main urban hubs into the new century. With the modern new bridges in New Orleans (1935) and Baton Rouge (1940) and the completion of U. S. Highway 61 connecting the two cities, one no longer had to follow the twists and turns of the Mississippi River Road. But as natural resources were promoted and at times squandered, notions of historic preservation took a backseat to the ideals of modernity and progress.

As the United States entered World War II, Baton Rouge and the petrochemical empire began to grow so intensely that great changes could be observed by anyone returning after a departure of only a few months. The Mississippi River's role as a primary lifeline for goods and materials became critical to the war effort, and the region's importance would be maintained throughout the Cold War. New Orleans has maintained its preeminent role as a world port and still transports the largest tonnage in the world.

While the River Road steadily industrialized, it developed an almost contrary character as an inspiration to artists and writers. Around 1900, the Woodward brothers, who founded the School of Architecture at Tulane University and the Art Department of the Newcomb College for Women, felt that the old architecture and landscape of New Orleans and the River Road should serve as a progenitor of new architecture and art. Leaders in the early movement of regionalism in the arts, the Woodwards

regularly took their students on River Road field trips and led early battles for preservation, which came with increasing frequency. The ambience and heritage of a major cultural statement were in danger, but many guidebooks extolled the virtues of the Louisiana experience and helped to focus world attention on its importance and potential demise.

In the heady days of the 1920s and 1930s, artists and writers came from all over the world to experience the creative atmosphere of south Louisiana. The French Quarter and other neighborhoods of old New Orleans provided inexpensive accommodations, as well as food and drink of great character. Literati met and talked in the courtyards of New Orleans and took long drives along the River Road; nights turned into weeks as plantation settings gave sustenance to creative spirits. Many of these individuals created images and wrote books that promoted the importance of the River Road and its urban centers. In books such as *Old Louisiana*, Lyle Saxon celebrated the character and experience of the area; many of his works were illustrated by architect-artist E. H. Suydam. In 1945, Harnett T. Kane wrote *Plantation Parade: The Grand Manner in Louisiana* and established the River Road as one of the most popular settings for literature in the post–World War II era. Important photographers such as Edward Weston and Clarence John Laughlin photographed the River Road. Laughlin's poignant photographs and poetic descriptions created the most important published statement to date—*Ghosts Along the Mississippi: The Magic of the Old Houses of Louisiana*. George Washington Cable, Walt Whitman, Francis Parkinson Keyes, William Faulkner, Tennessee Williams, Howard Roark, and Sherwood Anderson are but a few of the great writers of the past who found inspiration in the life and times of the River Road. The tradition they established continues today with authors such as Anne Rice, who has created some of the most intense images ever written about this region.

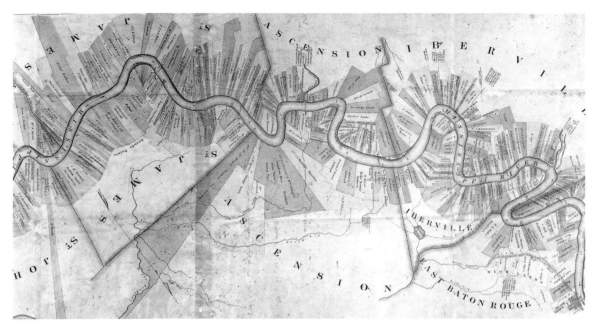

A section of the plat map Norman's Chart of the Lower Mississippi River, *by architect and civil engineer Marie Adrien Persac and published in 1858. The plantation parcels between New Orleans and Baton Rouge are delineated and identified by their owner of that time. (Courtesy of Louisiana State University Special Collections, Hill Memorial Library.)*

In the 1930s and '40s, many wealthy patrons began to purchase historic properties and restore them as personal settings for intellectual salons and for the sheer pleasure the plantation context provided. Many of these same individuals began the fight for historic preservation. The Louisiana Landmarks Society, the Foundation for Historical Louisiana, the River Road Historical Society, and the Louisiana Preservation Alliance are all organizations formed in response to the degradation of historic environments between Baton Rouge and New Orleans. Today, almost every parish, town, and city has a preservation organization.

In the 1990s, the National Trust for Historic Preservation listed the River Road as one of the most endangered historic sites in the United States. The Historic American Buildings Survey, founded during the Great Depression, had focused its initial attention on this same region, and that attention continues through the development of preservation programs at the Tulane University School of Architecture and the University of New Orleans College of Urban and Public Affairs. Most of the other universities and colleges of Louisiana have some form of preservation studies program. In 1977, the Education through Historic Preservation Program focused attention on the need for heritage education along the River Road for young students and their families.

Historically, changes in transportation and cargo technology precipitated changes in the river system in both urban and rural areas. Many of these changes, as well as changes in the levee protection system itself, contributed to the demise of important eighteenth- and nineteenth-century landmarks. In some cases, plantation principal houses had to be moved as the levee was increased in vertical and horizontal dimension; in others, the great structures and their related outbuildings were destroyed. Uncle Sam Plantation is possibly the most unfortunate example of this destruction. At Uncle Sam, even the outbuildings were built in the boldest Greek Revival design, and Clarence John Laughlin felt that Uncle Sam represented the best example of Louisiana's interpretation of classical architecture. If it were with us today, it would be one of the most important nineteenth-century landmarks in the world.

The Civil War caused the destruction of many plantations—directly through bombardment and fire and indirectly through the economic situation of the aftermath. Fire was the cause for the demise of many plantations—Belmont, Longview, Belle Grove, Elmwood, Le Petit Versailles, and The Cottage are just a few. Sarpy and Evan Hall Plantations were destroyed by the Mississippi River itself as it ate away the very land under their foundations. Angelina, Prospect, Myrtleland, Gypsy, California, Sport, Zenon Trudeau, Helvetia, Linwood, Chatsworth, Dunboyne, Killona and Waterford Plantations comprise a short list of landmarks that were demolished as the result of one form of progress or another.

Either directly or indirectly, industry has been responsible for the destruction of many plantation settings. Although the Marathon Oil Company bulldozed Welham Plantation, it was forced to maintain San Francisco Plantation as a sale requirement from the Ingram Oil Company. The problem of preservation also extends to elements of the natural landscape. The Locke Breaux Oak, for example, was the grandfather of all live oak trees extant in twentieth-century Louisiana. Its branches spread in all directions, covering the equivalent of a city block, but it was destroyed by Hooker Chemical to create a parking lot. After it was cut, its rings were read to reveal an age of over a thousand years. Man, in his obsession for control, had taken in one quick and thoughtless act what it had taken nature a millennium to create.

At times, destruction has come as a result of the historical plantation system itself. Crescent Farm Plantation was formed by the uniting of two adjacent Creole settings, Robichaux and Hymel. It still exists in the original family ownership, but the principal houses were allowed to be torn down for their lumber; the owning family had become so large that no one was able to organize a viable effort to save the structures. The old Louisiana property inheritance laws tended to create these unmanageable land holdings, which over time came to have too many owners and too little organizational control. Recent changes in the law, however, should alleviate some of these problems.

The Louisiana legislature has given permission to cities to create historic district and landmark commissions, but it has forbidden nonincorporated areas and specific sites from having similar protection. Until this legal situation is changed, the majority of the River Road sites have no legal protection. This remains the single most important reason to fear for the future of historic plantation architecture.

One of the most critical reasons for the continuing destruction of the cultural heritage of the River Road is a lack of caring by the citizens and families who control the rules and regulations of ownership and responsibility. The governing idea is that there are so many historic properties that the loss of one would not be missed, but the losses have increased to the point that very few properties are left. Some people who have grown up in the hard life of plantation culture of recent times see the houses as symbols of a way of life they do not value. Others see the big houses and their settings as representative of the time of slavery and do not want to keep the structures as viable memories, but this attitude discounts the fact that these great examples of architecture and landscape were built by master craftspeople, many of them slaves or free people of color, and are a tribute to their genius, too. Without these vestiges of our past, we go into the next century without a context of who we are and where we have been.

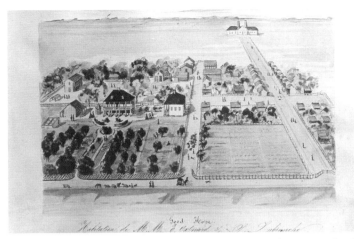

In this 1859 painting by Father Michael Joseph Paret, the priest at St. Charles of Borromeo Church, the elaborate
arrangement of buildings at Good Hope Plantation is eloquently depicted. Today there is no trace
of any of this village-like setting. Good Hope was inundated by the river in the 1860s and never rebuilt.
(Reproduced by permission of Marcel Boyer, Visages de notre Pilat, *Pélussin, France.)*

The past will not go without a fight. A growing population of preservationists understands that a sense of place and a sense of the past are necessary for the maintenance of a personal and societal culture. Without the context of one's history, the image and identity of a society ceases to exist. Just as the French language has been the vehicle to maintain the continuity of Creole and Acadian life in Louisiana, the natural and built environment provides the physical and spiritual strength for historical and environmental preservation.

The Great Mississippi River Road between Baton Rouge and New Orleans is a very special place. Nowhere else in the New World have humanity, culture, nature, technology, and change fought and coexisted so powerfully. Millions visit every year. They express their sorrow that so much is gone as well as their joy that what is left is so unique and special. It becomes harder every year to develop cultural tourism along this great stretch of water and roadway; yet as the experience becomes increasingly poignant, it must be preserved. One hopes the vestiges of this cultural phenomenon will inspire the human commitment that will ensure its preservation.

EUGENE CIZEK, PH.D. FAIA

Professor of Architecture and Latin American Studies
Director of Preservation Studies
Tulane School of Architecture

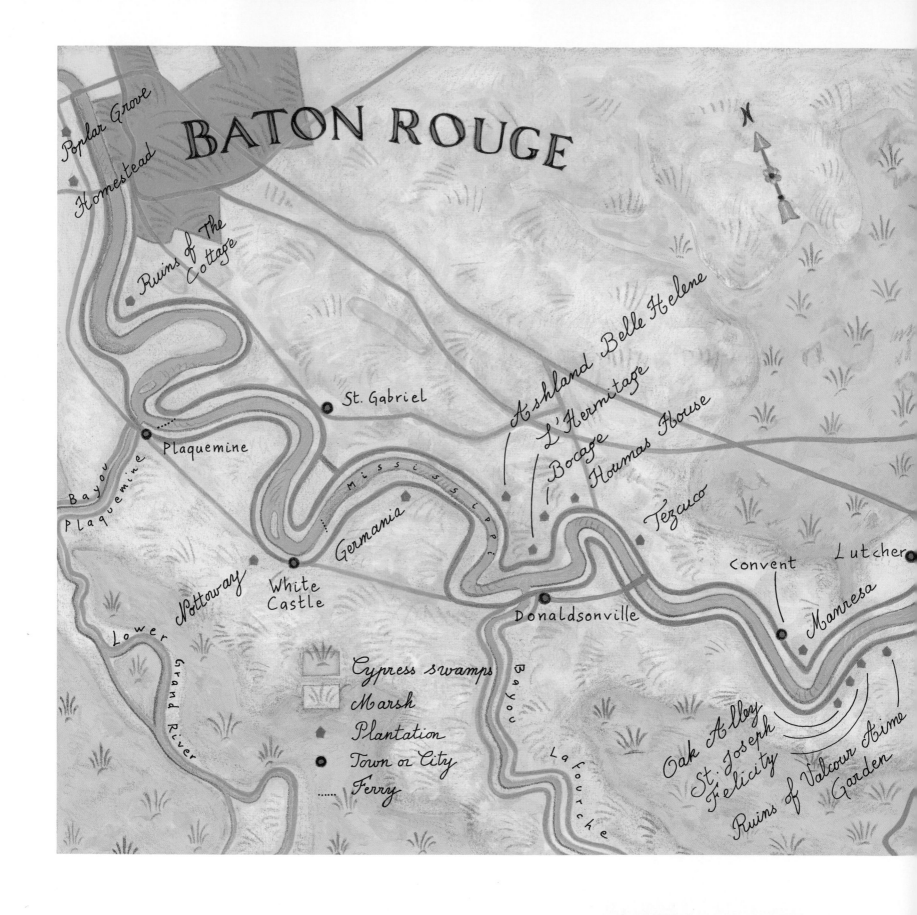

Lake Maurepas
Lake Pontchartrain
NEW ORLEANS
10
San Francisco
LaPlace
Ormond
Destrehan
Elmwood Site
Magnolia Lane
Edgard
Gramercy
Haydel-Jones
Glendale
River
Home Place
Evergreen
Whitney
Laura
Desiré
Vacherie
Lake Des Allemands
Lake Salvador

THE PATTERN OF SETTLEMENT

CHAPTER ONE

"It is of the utopia of before the war that old southerners speak. It was here and it is gone. The best of all possible worlds existed in the south and it was destroyed. And, truly, if merely a part of this remembered grandeur once existed in reality, Louisiana plantation life must have been almost paradisiacal."

LYLE SAXON
Gumbo Ya-Ya: Folk Tales of Louisiana
1945

At the core of the River Road settlement pattern were the narrow land concessions instituted by the French during the colonial period to maximize river frontage. Collectively, this pattern has been likened to that of a linear village, but other patterns were embedded within it. Each narrow concession defined an individual plantation that was itself a planned community—a largely self-sufficient, rural compound. It was village-like, with ensembles of outbuildings in proximity to the principal house and rows of slave cabins further back. Residential buildings were complemented by an array of farm buildings, the most significant of which was the sugarhouse, where cane juice was laboriously extracted, distilled into molasses, and then crystallized into raw sugar.

The pattern cannot be described solely as plantation villages strung together in linear fashion like pearls on a necklace, however. There were also churches and country cemeteries, steamboat landings, and discrete towns such as Donaldsonville—the one-time state capital—and Plaquemine and White Castle, among numerous other smaller hamlets. Together these components formed the pattern of settlement of the River Road.

A common River Road settlement pattern unfolds in this view looking upriver along the east bank in the community of Convent. The river's edge, heavily laden with barges, meets its natural bank, the batture. Behind the batture is the massive levee maintained by the U. S. Army Corps of Engineers. At the levee's base is the River Road. The houses of Convent face the road in a linear pattern. In the background is the spire of St. Michael's Catholic Church, with a petrochemical complex beyond.

In a setting that is prototypical of River Road plantation sites, St. Joseph Plantation House majestically faces the river. Forward of the principal house is the River Road, levee, and batture. To the sides are auxiliary residential and farm buildings. In the flat open fields behind the plantation complex are long rows of sugarcane ready for harvest.

THE PATTERN OF SETTLEMENT

Bon Sejour, more commonly known as Oak Alley, is framed by an ancient gnarled arcade of live oaks, forming an auspicious axis between house and river. This *allée* of twenty-eight live oaks was about a hundred years old when Jacques Telesphore Roman chose this site to build Bon Sejour in the late 1830s. The trees had been planted by an unknown French settler early in the eighteenth century to frame the river vista of a modest colonial structure. The Romans thus enjoyed the rarity of a mature *allée* of live oaks for their new house. *Allées* of trees were a common landscaping element that created shady pathways and dramatic vistas between the principal house of the plantation and the river.

The privy at Evergreen, with its Greek Revival pilasters and pediment, stands as a diminutive temple monument to nineteenth-century human hygiene. The secondary buildings at Evergreen have withstood the ravages of time because they were so substantially built, of masonry rather than wood.

RIGHT

At Evergreen Plantation, in St. John Parish just above the community of Edgard, the back of the principal house faces a formal parterre garden bordered by a kitchen building on the right, the plantation office on the left, and, to the rear, the privy. This ensemble, built as part of a major remodeling of Evergreen in 1832, is typical of the compound-like character of plantation sites. Planters were noted for constructing a separate building for every need they had. In the grander settings, such as this one, a village-like setting ultimately emerged. Creoles frequently employed the formal French parterre as a landscaping device to link the secondary structures at the rear of the principal house.

In a less-formal arrangement than at Evergreen, these secondary residences at St. Joseph Plantation are sited behind the principal house. At least one of these structures was moved to this site in contemporary times. The overseer's house was frequently to the side of the principal house, commonly facing the side road leading to the slave cabins in the rear. In this instance, the overseer's house is on the far left, directly behind and facing the principal house. As families grew, or became extended, it was common practice to build separate residences near the principal house to accommodate the need for more living space.

RIGHT
It was customary on Creole plantations to provide separate living quarters for male children as they began to mature to adulthood. These buildings were referred to as *garçonnières*, which translates literally as "boy's place." In practice, such buildings might have a variety of uses, like guesthouses. Houmas House has two unique *garçonnières* of hexagonal shape with pointed ogee roofs capped by a finial. They are largely ornamental, offering little living space. Each has a tiny sitting room below and a bedroom above. They functioned as garden houses.

One of the two *pigeonniers* at Whitney Plantation has survived. Creoles raised pigeons both as a source of food and for their guano, which was used for fertilizer for gardens. In France, only the landowning gentry were allowed to raise pigeons, so the presence of a *pigeonnier* ultimately became something of a status symbol. This cultural phenomenon migrated to south Louisiana, where principal houses were commonly flanked by pairs of distinctive, and frequently highly ornamented, *pigeonniers*.

RIGHT

This marginally surviving structure at Home Place is a rare hybrid form—a combination *pigeonnier* and carriage house dating from about 1800. In the early twentieth century, the carriage house below was used to store a family buggy; it ultimately became a storage shed for farm equipment. Lacking any contemporary use, it is now abandoned and seriously deteriorating.

A late-eighteenth-century Creole barn still stands at Whitney Plantation. It is thought that this barn, whose framing, proportion, and steeply sloped pavilion roof are all indicative of French colonial traditions, might predate the principal house of about 1800. Farm buildings were commonly sited behind the living complex and in front of the fields. This one is unusually close to the principal house, a fact that may have contributed to its survival. Even though it is a barn, it has a raised foundation to prevent flooding.

A storage shed near the principal house at Whitney. Specialized structures were characteristic of the plantation compound, and of the planter's predilection to have separate structures for specific uses.

On the east bank, in the town of LaPlace, is Amelie (also known as the J. O. Montegut house), a modest Creole house surrounded in the traditional manner by *pieux* fencing consisting of pointed, rough-hewn cypress planks stuck into the ground. The grounds of Creole plantation buildings were traditionally fenced in this vernacular manner, with secondary buildings frequently having smaller fences of their own.

RIGHT

Germania Plantation features elaborate outbuildings, including this carriage house, built about 1890, complete with a ventilating cupola and carpenter Gothic ornamentation. It is rare for utilitarian buildings other than *pigeonniers*, which were considered status symbols and embellishments to the principal house, to reflect such high style. Published sources have mistakenly described this building as a plantation church, confusing the cupola for a church spire and presuming a greater level of importance based on its architectural detailing.

A portion of a chimney stack and a vine-covered front facade are all that remain of a worker cabin at Magnolia Lane Plantation. A house servant, the cook at the principal house, had resided there as recently as 1980.

LEFT
A dirt road perpendicular to the River Road on the west bank in St. James Parish forms the division between Felicity and St. Joseph plantations. In the distance is a worker cabin. Roads perpendicular to the river became a common corridor of secondary development, typically leading to slave cabins or, in the postbellum era, sharecropper or worker cabins. The primary pattern of linear development along the river was complemented by tangentially configured secondary uses.

OVERLEAF
At Evergreen Plantation, an intact slave-cabin site has miraculously survived—a melancholic vestige of the institution of slavery. Neat rows of wooden double cabins are precisely aligned along an oak-shrouded lane. Each cabin accommodated two families. Slave cabin sites, referred to as "the quarters," were characterized by their village-like arrangement. This siting arrangement, with the cabins aligned perpendicular to the River Road and well back from the river, is typical of River Road plantations.

In the nineteenth century, every plantation provided for its own sugar processing and therefore had a sugar-house, typically sited behind the barns and residential outbuildings, or amid the cane fields. In the early twentieth century, major consolidations driven by economic factors took place. Larger sugarhouses serving several plantations became the norm. The sugarhouse at Germania Plantation, now in ruins, was last used before World War I. Idle for decades, the stack is now covered with vines, the building's roof has collapsed, and its elaborate Victorian machinery is askew amid encroaching weeds and vines.

In contrast to the smaller nineteenth-century sugarhouses, which served a single plantation, the St. James Sugar Cooperative is a much larger, modern facility serving cane farmers throughout the region.

The process of making crystallized sugar from cane juice is an elaborate one. Juice is first extracted from the cane stalk and concentrated via a distillation process and then filtered to remove impurities. This process is called clarification. Afterward, raw sugar is crystallized from the thick, clarified syrup, or molasses, which is then "purged" of the residual molasses, so that only cooled, crystallized sugar remains. This raw sugar product is then sold to the sugar refineries to be made into white, refined sugar. There are only two remaining sugar refineries in all of south Louisiana, the Colonial Sugar Refinery in Gramercy and the Domino Sugar Refinery in Chalmette.

This housing cluster is an example of development tangential to the River Road. Working-class communities, often black, tended to adopt this pattern, utilizing cheaper land lacking river frontage rather than spreading out in linear fashion along the River Road itself.

During the antebellum period, the river was the true highway for the planters. The River Road—unpaved, heavily rutted, and frequently flooded—could only support local traffic. In 1812, the steamboat era began and in the ensuing years steamboats carrying cargo and passengers plied the great river relentlessly. Landings were established along the river for scheduled boarding and the taking on and unloading of cargo.

The Caire Landing in Edgard, which dates from about 1860, was moved to its current site in 1881 to accommodate a levee setback. Long after passenger and cargo travel on the river had subsided, showboats stopped twice a year at Caire Landing through the 1930s. Today the Landing building stares blankly out to the levee while autos line up to cross by ferry to the town of Reserve, on the east bank. Fixtures from the Caire Store, the plantation store for Church Place Plantation, are stored inside the landing building. In its day one of the largest stores for miles along the River Road, the Caire Store closed in the 1970s, no longer able to compete with the burgeoning retailers in the outlying suburban areas of New Orleans and Baton Rouge. The building remains in the Caire family, owned by the grandson of E. J. Caire.

St. Philip Catholic Church and Cemetery, on the west bank in Vacherie, illustrates the typical pattern for religious buildings: The church building faced the river, and the cemetery would be either to the side or behind it. A settlement and sense of community would frequently coalesce around the church building, as has occurred here.

RIGHT

In St. Gabriel, on the east bank, is the old St. Gabriel Catholic Church. Whereas St. Gabriel appears to be a typical late-nineteenth-century Gothic church building, recent research indicates that it is actually a much older structure that was later refashioned in the Gothic style. Beneath the Gothic veneer are the bones of a French colonial-type structure erected during the Spanish period between 1774 and 1776. St. Gabriel served as a church for Acadians, who were being settled in this area to thwart further advances of the English, who had settled just upriver. This is the only church in Louisiana originally of French colonial construction known to have survived.

The Catholic Church was a pervasive presence on the River Road, as in all of south Louisiana. It divided the Louisiana colony into parishes of Catholic control that have survived as political units to the present. Country churches with adjacent cemeteries were a fundamental element around which communities developed and are an important part of the River Road experience today.

THE PATTERN OF SETTLEMENT

This imposing classical edifice in Convent was once the home of the College of Jefferson, established in 1831 by River Road planters to provide for the local education of their children. Named for Thomas Jefferson, the college was noted for its library, museum of natural history, science laboratories, and decorative paintings. Though the college boasted this elegant, grandly scaled structure, the handsome edifice belied early financial woes. The state of Louisiana withdrew financial support in 1845, and the school closed due to bankruptcy in 1848. Noted Creole planter Valcour Aime purchased the college in 1859 and reopened it, then in 1864 Aime donated the school to the Marist Fathers, who continued to operate it until 1927 as St. Mary's Jefferson College. In 1931, the Jesuit Fathers of New Orleans rescued it from potential oblivion, reestablishing the site as Manresa Retreat House, a spiritual retreat for lay people.

Manresa's contemporary appearance is largely the result of a Classical Revival remodeling in the 1840s following a fire. Manresa is quite rare historically because very little architecture of a civic nature ever existed on the River Road. Its survival to the present makes it all the more unique.

Donaldsonville—A River Road town about midway between New Orleans and Baton Rouge. Life on the River Road was not entirely a rural experience. Small, discrete towns developed, typically at the confluences of secondary waterways and the river. Such is the case with Donaldsonville, which is sited at the confluence of Bayou Lafourche and the Mississippi. The town was founded by William Donaldson in 1806 and was given his name in 1822. Donaldsonville briefly functioned as the state capital during the 1829–30 legislative session, before Baton Rouge became the capital. It retains much of the character of a small nineteenth-century town.

RIGHT

Occupying an entire block of Mississippi Street, as the River Road is named in its Donaldsonville stretch, is the mercantile establishment of Bernard Lemann & Brothers Inc. This handsome Italianate building was built in 1876 and designed by noted New Orleans architect William Freret. The current Lemann Brothers store now operates across the street, and this historic building has been recently converted to a museum.

A house detail and a streetscape on Lessard Street, in downtown Donaldsonville, convey a nineteenth-century small-town ambience.

These weathered shotgun cottages with Eastlake detailing are on Lessard Street in Donaldsonville between William and Charles Streets. They currently serve as tenements for black families and in all likelihood were originally built for that purpose.

Plaquemine, sited at the confluence of Bayou Plaquemine and the river, is just below Baton Rouge on the west bank. Originally subdivided by Thomas Pipkin as the town of Iberville, it was renamed after the bayou on incorporation in 1838. *Plaquemine* is the Indian word for the local persimmon, which grows in abundance in the area. In the nineteenth century, Bayou Plaquemine was an important commercial waterway, but its access to the river was problematic due to the levee and the variances in the water levels between the river and the bayou. This prompted the construction of the Plaquemine Lock—seen on the left. The lock was completed in 1909, designed by George Goethals, the future chief engineer of the Panama Canal.

This elegant Greek Revival edifice, directly across the street from the Plaquemine Lock, was originally constructed in 1849 as the Iberville Parish Courthouse. It subsequently became the Plaquemine City Hall. It now serves as the chamber of commerce offices and as a tourist information center.

RIGHT
The American flag hangs from the front gallery of a center hall cottage on Plaquemine's Eden Street.

Not all grand antebellum residences on the River Road were located on plantations. The elegant Middleton house in Plaquemine, built about 1845, is at the corner of Eden and Plaquemine Streets.

In the community of Wallace, on the west bank of St. John Parish, is Whitney Plantation. Jean Jacques Haydel built the principal house at Whitney about 1800 in the Creole tradition, with brick construction on the first floor and brick-between-post construction on the main living floor above. The house has not been occupied for about twenty years. The site is currently owned by Formosa Plastics, a Taiwanese firm that purchased the site as the potential location for a rayon plant. Formosa is in the process of selling the portion of the parcel on which the numerous historic structures are located.

The Creole plantation house, though quite sophisticated, represented a vernacular form, and it was once pervasive. John Latrobe, the son of architect Benjamin Latrobe, observed in his travel journals that "the plantation houses. . . . in this part of the world appear to have been built, all of them, after the same model. . . . The climate requires all the shade that can be procured, and to obtain it the body of the building is surrounded by galleries."

Home Place Plantation is on the west bank, in the community of Hahnville in St. Charles Parish. It was built about 1800 for Pierre Gaillard or his widow, possibly by the Creole of color Charles, who built Destrehan. Home Place is a classic example of the Creole tradition in plantation residences, which featured a heavy timber frame with mortise and tenon construction, and a steeply pitched, heavy frame roof. The frame would typically rest on massive brick piers, or a brick, above-ground basement of sufficient height to constitute a full story. The principal living space was the timber-framed second story, in the manner of a *piano nobile*—the principal floor of a large villa with formal reception area and dining rooms, one flight above the ground floor. Home Place has a masonry ground floor, constructed of plantation-made bricks, incorporating a wine cellar. The main floor above is framed with cypress timber and infilled with *bousillage*, a mixture of river mud, Spanish moss, and animal hair held together by horizontal slats or laths.

Today, Home Place is owned by the Keller family, whose ownership began in 1889 when Pierre Anatole Keller bought out the interest of his father-in-law, Damion Haydel. In 1904, major renovations were made by Theodore P. Keller. Other than this remodeling and the addition of a new red metal roof about 1990, Home Place is remarkably intact. The house was last occupied as a residence in the 1980s.

RIGHT

A detail of the side gallery at Home Place illustrates the manner in which Creole plantation houses were detailed. Massive lower masonry columns of simplified Doric or Tuscan order support the gallery floor. Much lighter turned, wooden colonettes support the roof overhang above. A slight flare at the eave line is an embellishment associated with the Creole building tradition. The carriage beneath the lower gallery was placed there in the 1980s; a local doctor once used it for making house calls.

Destrehan is on the east bank, in St. Charles Parish, in the community that is its namesake. The house was built between 1787 and 1790 by Charles, a Creole of color, for Robin de Logny. In 1802, the house was purchased by de Logny's son-in-law Jean Noel Destrehan, the owner with whom the house has long been identified. Destrehan is the grandest and earliest Creole plantation house surviving on the River Road to be fully documented. Originally the galleries were detailed in the Creole manner, with heavy masonry columns below and lighter turned colonettes above, but in the 1840s Destrehan was classicized in a major remodeling to conform to the Greek Revival style that had come into vogue. The side wings were added to create more living space in 1812. Many early Creole plantations were remodeled during the 1830s and 1840s to make them more fashionable.

Today Destrehan is owned by the River Road Historical Society, which has been gradually restoring the house, a process that is now near completion. Destrehan is open to the public as a house museum with guided tours.

Magnolia Lane Plantation is on the west bank in Jefferson Parish, just below the Huey P. Long Bridge at Nine Mile Point—a navigational marking nine miles upriver from Jackson Square in New Orleans. The principal house was built in the early 1800s in a style evocative of the West Indies. After a 1915 hurricane, the house was remodeled, including rebuilt galleries and a new roof. The house is *bousillage* construction on the main level over a masonry base. The floor plan consists of four parlors on either side of a grand center hall, with a loggia flanked by two *cabinet* at the rear. The dominant influences of Magnolia Lane are Creole, but the center hall plan shows Anglo influence. Hybrid elements are typical of south Louisiana building traditions.

Francis Quinette purchased the house from Edgar Fortier in 1867, and Quinette descendants still own it today. Originally known as the Fortier place, Magnolia Lane's acreage was small—about two hundred acres—though it remains intact to this day. The Quinettes used the acreage as a nursery for oaks and native plants. Francis Quinette supplied and planted the live oak seedlings for St. Charles Avenue, Audubon Park, and Tulane University in New Orleans.

Laura Plantation is on the west bank in the community of Vacherie in St. James Parish. The principal house at Laura was built by slave labor in 1805 by Guillaume DuParc on the site of a Colapissa Indian settlement. Despite embellishments of folk Victorian detailing added in 1905, Laura is very much a Creole building in type. The masonry constructed lower floor was used as a wine cellar and for storage. The main floor is brick-between-posts, originally stuccoed, and later covered with cypress weatherboards. The side galleries were enclosed in 1822. The house was originally U-shaped, with the rear wings enclosing a courtyard. At the rear of the U, a separate building housed the original kitchen. In 1922, the metal terra-cotta-painted roof replaced the original roof of cypress shingles, and the chimneys were clipped and roofed over. The house is about 17,000 square feet, including galleries, basement and attic. The attic framing incorporates Norman trusses.

Laura is named after Laura Locoul, the great-granddaughter of the builder, and is the oldest extant plantation complex in St. James Parish. Historian Alcée Fortier (grandson of Valcour Aime) recorded the folk tales of the Senegalese slaves at Laura and neighboring plantations. Fortier published the stories, passed down by French patois-speaking slaves, in his book *Folk Tales of Louisiana*. Essentially the same folk tales would be immortalized in English a decade later by Joel Chandler Harris in his Uncle Remus stories.

Today the principal house and historic secondary buildings at Laura are leased by the Laura Plantation Company, LLC, a for-profit group spearheaded by Norman and Sand Marmillion. A ten-year restoration program was begun in 1994, and the house has been converted to a museum offering daily tours.

Desiré is behind Laura in south Vacherie, adjacent to the *chemin militaire* (a ridge of high ground once used as a roadbed). Though Desiré was well behind the River Road, it had access to the river via the old, French military roadbed—a fine example of how smaller plantations could still maintain vital river access. The modest principal house (circa 1830s) is of the Acadian style. It is *bousillage* constructed on raised brick piers, stuccoed on the front, with weatherboards on the sides. In 1863, Phillippe Desiré LeBlanc purchased the property. From 1889 to about 1915, he ran a general store in a room cobbled onto the older house. LeBlanc grew perique tobacco on Desiré and received a license to make cigars in 1891. The cultivation of perique tobacco is an old cottage industry on the River Road. This tobacco is quite pungent and is typically blended with other tobaccos to impart an exotic flavor.

When the current owners, Michael and Claudette Davis, purchased Desiré in 1981, it was derelict, abandoned, and still owned by the descendants of LeBlanc. They began a long process of restoration that continues today. Wisely, the Davises have kept much of the patina of Desiré, which is a rare vestige of the perique tobacco industry in Louisiana—leading to the placement of this house on the National Register in 1986.

This modest four-room Creole cottage on Homestead Plantation is believed to have originally been the overseer's residence. It has been moved twice due to levee setbacks and is now sited with its lower side facing the River Road; the main entrance faces the cross street. It was built sometime between 1850 and the 1860s.

Overseer's houses were typically the most significant plantation residence after the principal house or planter's residence. Even so, there tended to be a rather steep declension in architectural scale and appointment between the residences of planter and overseer.

RIGHT

St. Joseph Plantation is on the west bank just below Oak Alley in St. James Parish. The principal house was built in 1820 by Dr. Cazamie Mericq. In 1847, the house was purchased by Alexis Ferry and his wife, Josephine Aime, one of Valcour Aime's daughters. Ferry remodeled the house in 1858, enclosing the first floor and adding two rooms on each end. In addition, the Creole house was given classical details, such as the Greek key doorway and the Doric box columns supporting the gallery. After Ferry, the house was sold to Edward Gay, who owned St. Louis Plantation, just below Plaquemine, and then in 1877 to Joseph Waguespack, who named it after his patron saint. St. Joseph is still owned by members of the Waguespack family today. The house has been unoccupied since 1997, and the Waguespack family is currently considering plans for making the house open to the public, either as a house museum or as a bed-and-breakfast accommodation.

Felicity Plantation is on the west bank, in St. James Parish. The principal house was built in 1847 by Valcour Aime as a wedding gift to his daughter Félicité and her husband, Septime Fortier. The house, with its classical detailing, combines Creole and Anglo influences. In 1899, the plantation was acquired by Saturnin Waguespack, who consolidated it in 1901 with St. Joseph, the adjoining upriver plantation already owned by the Waguespack family. Today Felicity is owned by the St. Joseph P & M Company Ltd., whose shareholders include members of the Waguespack family, who use the house as a full-time family residence.

Glendale Plantation is on the west bank in St. John Parish, near the St. Charles Parish line. The contemporary Glendale Plantation is a consolidation of the historical Glendale Plantation with the adjoining Hymelia and Kenmore Plantations. The principal house is essentially a raised Creole plantation house, though it contains numerous transitional influences, particularly after a pre–Civil War renovation, and reflects both Creole and Anglo sensibilities. The house was built about 1802 by David Paine and then remodeled incorporating numerous classical details. Originally the roof slope facing the river was embellished with two dormers, but these were removed in a contemporary remodeling. The Lanaux family acquired Glendale in 1922. In 1946, Denis Lanaux took over the cane business and lived in the principal house until 1953, when he built a new house nearby. Since 1953, Glendale has been used for family gatherings, weddings, and weekend visits by family members.

RIGHT

The front gallery at Glendale looks out to the river and catches its cooling breezes. The gallery is an integral component of River Road plantation houses, particularly ones such as Glendale with Creole floor plans that have no interior halls. The gallery is used both as a corridor of circulation and to shade the interiors from the blistering south Louisiana sun.

Bocage Plantation is on the east bank of the river between the communities of Burnside and Darrow. *Bocage*, French for "shady retreat," was built in 1801 by prominent Creole planter Marius Pons Bringier for his fourteen-year-old daughter, Francoise, and her husband, Christoph Colomb. This house was originally a raised Creole house—brick on the first floor supporting a heavy-timber frame above—but it was completely redesigned in the Greek Revival style after a fire in 1837. The renovating architect is believed to have been James Dakin of New Orleans. Eight square plastered brick columns support a massive entablature with an encircling dentil course. These sophisticated details along with the interior plaster moldings on the second floor are typical of designs executed by Dakin for houses in New Orleans.

Bocage is now the private residence of the heirs of Dr. Anita Crozat Kohlsdorf, who purchased the house in 1942 and restored it.

Ashland was built in 1842 by one of the most prominent sugar planters, and a later-to-be Confederate legislator, Duncan Farrar Kenner. Twenty-eight massive columns, each three feet square, support an austere Greek Revival entablature. Ashland has been attributed to New Orleans architect James Gallier, Sr., though no written historical corroboration is known to exist. Stylistically, Ashland resembles the work of James Dakin, who was known for using heavy rectangular columns in his designs. It is not far-fetched, however, to presume that a wealthy, well-traveled, and headstrong client such as Duncan Kenner might have placed his predilections in the hands of his builder, bypassing the services of an architect altogether. In fact, photographs have been recently uncovered of a long-demolished twin, Terre aux Lillas, in the community of Belle Rose, on Bayou Lafourche, just below Donaldsonville. The twin was built about 1851 and appears to be an unabashed copy of Ashland executed by a builder—evidence that sophisticated buildings come about in many ways and do not always involve the participation of a talented architect.

In 1889, Ashland was purchased by John Reuss, a German émigré. Reuss saw the birth of a granddaughter, Helene, soon after the purchase and was prompted to change the name of the plantation to Belle Helene. The plantation is now known by the compound name—Ashland/Belle Helene.

OVERLEAF

Evergreen Plantation house is on the west bank in St. John the Baptist Parish above the community of Edgard. The principal house was built about 1800 by the same family that built Whitney upriver, and the two principal houses were originally almost identical. In 1832, Evergreen was classicized in a major remodeling by then-owner Pierre Becnel that included the addition of the substantial outbuildings, all of which have survived. The belvedere on the roof and the two-storied columns date from the 1832 remodeling.

By the late 1920s, Evergreen, having been through a succession of owners, fell into disrepair. In 1944, Matilda Gray of New Orleans and Lake Charles purchased the place and commenced a major restoration/remodeling. She used it as a weekend estate until her death. Her niece, Matilda Stream, owns the house today and has recently completed another major restoration of the house and grounds. This site, the most intact on the River Road, was opened to the public in the fall of 1998.

L'Hermitage is in Ascension Parish, on the east bank about a mile below the community of Darrow. Built by Michel Douradou Bringier, the building was begun in 1812 and completed in 1814. Bringier, who fought under Andrew Jackson in the Battle of New Orleans, named his house after Jackson's Tennessee estate. Jackson visited here in 1840 and perhaps earlier. It's possible that L'Hermitage is one of the very earliest classically detailed houses in Louisiana. While published sources have attributed the current appearance of the house to an 1840s remodeling—the presumption being that L'Hermitage was originally configured in the traditional Creole manner—recent restorations and repairs have not turned up any architectural evidence of such a remodeling. The current owners assert that the only alteration was the addition of a rear center wing in the late 1830s. If so, L'Hermitage could have been influential to the design of later houses, such as Oak Alley and Houmas House, and to the classicizing remodelings at such early plantations as Destrehan.

L'Hermitage had been abandoned for nearly two decades when its current owners, Dr. and Mrs. Robert Judice, purchased the derelict house in 1959 and commenced a gradual process of restoration and remodeling. Theodore Landry designed the contemporary landscaping in the 1960s. The entry gates came from the demolished Armant Plantation, across the river.

RIGHT

L'Hermitage is now graced by a young *allée* of live oaks planted by the Judices in 1992 using five-year-old seedlings. Today we are accustomed to the gnarly, fully mature oak *allées* framing views to the plantation house, but in the antebellum period, they were freshly planted and looked much like this *allée* at L'Hermitage.

Nottoway Plantation is on the west bank, just above the town of White Castle in Iberville Parish. New Orleans architect Henry Howard designed Nottoway for John Hampden Randolph, who named the plantation for the Nottoway River in his home state of Virginia. Nottoway, completed in 1859, with 53,000 square feet and sixty-four rooms, is an imposing pile with a mixture of Italianate and Greek Revival influences. In *Gumbo Ya-Ya*, Lyle Saxon described Nottoway as "a fortress calculated to defy the attacks of time and shelter a dozen generations of southern gentility yet unborn." Henry Howard's plans have never been found, leading to the speculation that perhaps Randolph destroyed them to thwart the likelihood of a similar house ever being built.

Though claims of grander relative scale are unsubstantiated, Nottoway is undeniably the largest extant antebellum structure on the River Road between New Orleans and Baton Rouge. A neighboring house, the now-demolished Belle Grove, was actually larger, but today Nottoway does not have a close second anywhere in its immediate vicinity. It is one of the last great pre–Civil War houses on the River Road, and represents something of a baroque conclusion to the antebellum affluence of the planter families.

Nottoway is currently open to the public with guided tours. It also functions as a bed-and-breakfast with a restaurant and meeting facilities on the site.

The front gallery on the third floor of Nottoway yields a vista over the top of the levee to the river and an island beyond. In the nineteenth century, virtually all the plantation principal houses had views of the river, but today almost none do because the levee has been raised so dramatically over the years.

San Francisco Plantation is on the east bank, in the community of Garyville in St. John the Baptist Parish. It was built by Edmond Marmillion in the 1850s and was completed shortly before his death in 1856. In a design that has been described as an eclectic mix of the new and the old-fashioned, San Francisco represents a baroque elaboration of the Creole plantation house. Stylistically, the house is a combination of Classical Revival and Gothic elements, but the floor plan is essentially Creole—a *piano nobile*, without hallways and with an enclosed rear loggia flanked by *cabinet*.

The name is a corruption of the French phrase *sans frusquin*, meaning "left without a cent," and is a reference to the cost of the highly elaborated house. Later the name became St. Frusquin and, finally, San Francisco. In the 1920s, the newly expanded levee was built around San Francisco thanks to the lobbying effort of one of the owners at that time, Sidney Levet, Sr., who saved the house from certain demolition. The house was restored between 1974 and 1977 by the New Orleans architectural firm of Koch & Wilson. The restoration was commissioned by ECOL Oil Company, which during restoration was purchased by Marathon Oil. Today the house is operated as a house museum by San Francisco Plantation Foundation.

LEFT

A view of the downriver side of San Francisco shows one of the two cisterns, each of which has a capacity of 8,000 gallons. The most common source of water on River Road plantations was cisterns, rather than wells. The extremely high water table in south Louisiana contaminated wells with muddy surface water.

Poplar Grove is on the west bank near the town of Port Allen, in West Baton Rouge Parish. The principal house began its life as the Banker's Pavilion for the 1884 World's Industrial and Cotton Centennial Exposition held in New Orleans. It was moved to Poplar Grove in 1886 by then-owner Joseph Harris. The pavilion was designed by Thomas Sully and exemplifies the influence of the aesthetic movement of the Victorian period. This movement incorporated Oriental motifs and early arts-and-crafts elements. Popular in England, it never attained critical mass in the United States and was exceedingly rare in south Louisiana. The house is now painted in a polychromatic color scheme intended to dramatize its aesthetic qualities.

From 1886, Horace Wilkinson managed the plantation and then purchased Poplar Grove in 1895. About 1915, Julia Merwin Wilkinson, Horace's wife, adjoined the former pavilion to an older four-room cottage already on the grounds, thus giving the house its current configuration.

After Horace Wilkinson's death in 1941, the house was vacated and essentially abandoned, but it was saved from vandalism and decay by Chauvin and Ruth Wilkinson, who purchased Poplar Grove from Horace's estate. Today their daughter, Ann Wilkinson, owns and lives in the house.

Germania Plantation is on the west bank, in Ascension Parish about ten miles above the town of Donaldsonville. The principal house was built by John Reuss about 1885 and was likely an addition to an older house rather than new construction. The style is essentially Eastlake. Descendants of John Reuss still own the property. They lived in the principal house until the early 1980s, but it is now unoccupied and in bad repair. The roof collapsed a few years ago. The service wing is still intact, although it has active roof leaks. While it is well on its way to becoming a ruin, at least a portion of the principal house at Germania could be saved if immediate measures were taken.

RIGHT

The Cottage Plantation is on the east bank in East Baton Rouge Parish, a few miles below Baton Rouge. The masonry columns of the lower story and foundations are the only remnants of an impressive Classical Revival principal house that burned to the ground in 1960 after being struck by lightning. The ruins are evocative of Vincent Scully's observation from *American Architecture and Urbanism:*

> "The scale of civilization and, indeed, of American frontier topography, was changing beyond the capacity of a temple form to control it. . . . [W]here those demands were least felt or most resisted, the old classic ideal could be longest retained in its romanticized form. The late Greek Revival plantation houses of the Deep South best embodied that condition and intention. Their softly gleaming column screens furnished the symbolic image around which Southern apologetics of the immediately pre–Civil War period and Southern mythology of the interminably postwar period were both to be fashioned. The more in ruin, the more Greek they seemed."

THE REALM OF THE INTERIOR

CHAPTER TWO

"And we find a house, a bright and resplendent habitation, which is not only an enchanted synthesis of all our mingled and multiformed remembrances of the loveliest and most cherished places we have known; but also, the very living symbol of our myriad search, our devious questing and constant loss, our fevered and persistent resumption of seeking again—for a true and final home in the dark and troubled chaos of the modern world."

CLARENCE JOHN LAUGHLIN

Ghosts along the Mississippi,

1948

Screened by colonnades and shuttered doorways, the interiors of the plantation houses, set in remote locations with private land all around, were veiled in mystery. Even by small-town standards, the planter and his family lived in isolation. Their most immediate neighbors were slaves, who held the peculiar entitlement of being both employee and property. The planter's only socioeconomic peers in this feudal society were his fellow planters. They may have been relatives, but they were also business competitors, or even archenemies, the coincidence of familial relation notwithstanding. The postbellum era changed this situation little—slaves became sharecroppers who ultimately would be replaced by machines. Life on the plantation remained one of relative seclusion.

In this environment, the home became monumental in significance. More than mere residence, it was also a place of business. Perhaps most significantly, it was a symbolic bastion poised against the wilderness—a place of civility in a swampy lowland perpetually vulnerable to the river's inundation. Those who live in plantation houses today have inherited much of the mystique of the planter's secluded chambers. Shelter, place of business, and status symbol rolled into one, the realm of the interior is the most intimate, inaccessible, vestige of plantation life.

A shuttered sash window in the *Maison de Reprise,* which literally translates as "retreat house" but is more descriptive as "dowager house." The *Maison* was built in 1829, behind and to the downriver side of the principal house at Laura, for Guillaume duParc's widow, Nanette Prud'Homme, who was retiring as president of the plantation. The structure has been abandoned since 1931 and awaits restoration.

RIGHT

The women's parlor at Laura. A unique feature of some Creole houses, such as Laura, was gender-specific parlors. The men's parlor was on the downriver side of the house facing New Orleans; the women's parlor was on the opposite, or upriver, side. These parlors allowed gender-based association and provided for the different roles that Creole society required of men and women.

On the mantel, to the right, is a *cylindre* or hurricane shade, a glass surround employed to prevent wind from blowing out the candlelight. Through the open doorway is the children's bedroom. Rollers on the beds allowed them to be rolled out to the gallery for sleeping in hot weather. At the foot of the bed is a baby bed used by the Waguespack family. The women's parlor served as the plantation office when women presidents ran the company.

The above-ground basement at Laura was used for storage only and incorporated a wine cellar. Many Creole families imported French wine both for their consumption and to sell. The basement contained fifteen racks for storing wine with a capacity of 10,000 bottles. The basement walls were plastered and the floor concreted in 1905.

Two olive jars were sunk into the ground in the basement floor. Sunken olive jars were common in Creole plantation houses, though their specific use has been lost to time. They may have been used as a secondary source for water storage, and since the water was cool, milk containers may have been submerged in them to help prevent the milk from spoiling.

RIGHT

A pair of French doors separates the dining room and main parlor at Laura. The Creole floor plan, which had no interior hallways, typically utilized the center, river-facing room as the main parlor. It was flanked by secondary parlors on either side.

The main parlor at Laura. The fireplace originally had a *faux marbre* finish. The cast-iron fireback also may have been original; if not, it likely dates from the remodeling in 1822. The chair on the right is the only item of furniture currently in the house that belonged to Laura Locoul. On the walls are remnants of the wallpaper from 1922. The first wallpapering of the house interiors was from 1822 and included this parlor and the dining room only. The traditional interior finish had been whitewashed plaster scored to resemble stone. There were three layers of wallpaper in this room, first from 1822, then 1905, and finally 1922. The doorway opens into the women's parlor.

Adjacent to the dining room is this pantry, where food was brought from the kitchen building for final preparation before serving. A trap door in this room once led to the wine cellar in the basement. In later years the room served as a storage room and a schoolroom.

RIGHT
The dining room at Laura, the largest room in the house, is behind the main parlor. In Creole floor plans, the dining room would typically be located here or in the center room of the ground floor. Originally there was a punkah above the dining table. A punkah is a large fan-shaped device that a servant would swing by pulling on an attached rope, thus creating a breeze.

DESTREHAN PLANTATION

The double parlors at Destrehan. The grand pocket doors with Greek key trim uniting the two rooms are from an 1840s remodeling. On the left is a portrait of Jean Noel Destrehan, on the right is a portrait of one of his daughters. The two classical mahogany gaming tables belonged to the Rost family. Pierre Rost, with his wife, Louise Odile (one of Destrehan's daughters) were the fourth owners of Destrehan.

The late empire gondola chairs are of the kind locally known as "Seignouret" after the New Orleans merchant who probably supplied them. Argand lamps are on the side tables and on the center table is a sinumbra (meaning "shadowless") lamp. The center gaming table made by Anthony G. Quervelle in Philadelphia was used in the entertainment of the Marquis de Lafayette during his 1830s visit to Louisiana.

RIGHT

Lydia's room is kept perpetually in summer dress with furnishings contemporary to about 1853, when Lydia Rost, daughter of Destrehan owner Emile Rost, died in this room in August—a victim of yellow fever.

The mantel painting is a late-1840s portrait of Lydia, believed to be by G. P. A. Healy. The rosewood *prie-dieu* dates from the 1850s. It is positioned at bedside for the priest's deliverance of the last rites. The rosewood commode is a Rost family piece. The bed, a mahogany, American-made full tester, late classical in style, dates from the 1830s. The bed coverings are handkerchief linen with Rost monograms.

Lydia's last rites were given by Father Paret, the priest at the Little Red Church, St. Charles of Borromeo, just upriver. Yellow fever was a horrific and pervasive disease that was dreaded throughout south Louisiana; Father Paret described Lydia's death in his journal, which roughly translated from the French read as follows: "The poor child is on the point of returning her soul to her Creator. She's suffered so much, spitting up black, rotten blood from her burning chest. Her whole body is covered with blisters. . . . Her haggard eyes seem to pop out of her head. Her cheeks are shrinking. Her teeth rattle and click against each other. . . . Her whole body twists and turns with such an unbelievable force that the doctor and I can barely hold her down. After a long and intense writhing, her pulse weakened and the agonizing death rattle began. Soon, we had only a corpse whose eyes I closed. That death will never be erased from my mind as long as I live . . . I could hardly remain standing and I trembled like a leaf . . . my eyes flooded with tears . . . Having finished this pious duty, they impose a second on me, that of announcing the news to the tearful family."

Between 1865 and 1867, this *cabinet* on the downriver side of Destrehan served as a local Freedman's Bureau office. In recognition of this use, the room is set up as it would have been during this period. An 1860s chromolithograph of Abraham Lincoln hangs above the 1840s fall-front desk. The office chair is from the same period. The clerk's desk behind is of cherry wood and dates from the 1850s. It is complemented by a bamboo Windsor chair. *Harper's Weekly*s from the mid 1860s are laid out on the desks.

All of the period settings in those rooms open to the public range from the 1820s to the 1860s and are based on a particular event or use from Destrehan's well-documented history. These rooms were curated by antiquarian Don Didier of New Orleans.

This is one of the rooms historically used as a family kitchen. The room may have also served as a laundry room at one time. The kitchen is arranged as it would have been for a *boucherie,* a traditional Creole hog butchering that included meat curing, sausage making, and so forth. The country table is American and is surrounded by Louisiana ladderback chairs. The sausage press is from the 1850s. A French Canadian chair sits in front of the hearth. In the fireplace, a roaster holds Louisiana ducks. The pigs' feet, laid out for preparation, were commonly used for glaces, sweet or hogshead cheese, and molded gelatins. Creole tomatoes have been placed on the windowsill for final ripening. The crockery is featheredge, green and white English pottery common to colonial Louisiana. Candle molds, French copper pots, and a drying rack for herbs and towels completes the ensemble.

Across the center hall from the parlor is the dining room. An eighteenth-century portrait hangs above the Sheraton sideboard, on which Old Paris porcelain from the 1830s is displayed. The English inlaid mahogany dining table is complemented by mahogany Louisiana-made gondola chairs. The chandelier overhead is a gasolier from the 1860s. The contemporary window treatments are based on a Federal design.

RIGHT

L'Hermitage, built in 1812 for the family of Michel Bringier, is a significant transitional house in that it wed Anglo influences—classical ornamentation and a Georgian-derived floor plan with formal rooms downstairs and bedrooms upstairs—to Creole preferences for French fenestrations and a prominent roof with ventilating dormers.

The parlor is downstairs, on the front upriver side of the center hall. European steel engravings of varied subjects adorn the wall above a Sheraton sewing table from the 1830s, which now serves as an end table to the Sheraton sofa adjacent. Flanking the sofa is a gondola-style mahogany chair.

The front bedroom on the downriver side of the house is used as the master bedroom. The mahogany full tester bed, which dates from 1830 or 1840, came from the New Iberia area. At the base of the bed is a walnut-stained cypress toolbox from the 1850s. In the foreground is a partial view of a *recamier,* or chaise longue covered in alligator hide.

SAN FRANCISCO PLANTATION

The gentlemen's parlor at San Francisco features a Bavarian hunting motif reflecting the sensibilities of owner Valsin Marmillion's German wife, Louise von Seybold. Valsin was the son of builder Edmond Marmillion, who died shortly after the house was completed. The Rococo Revival furniture is all of the period, but none is original to the house. The furniture was selected by Samuel Dornsife, a noted furniture historian and restoration consultant, in the mid-1970s restoration of San Francisco.

The ceiling murals, depicting the four seasons, were painted shortly after the house was completed. Based on an analysis of the brushstrokes, there were three muralists, most likely a master and two apprentices; historical references indicate they were Italian. Local tradition has it that Dominique Canova, an Italian immigrant artist then active in New Orleans, painted the murals, but this is unsubstantiated. If he did paint them, he did not do it single-handedly.

Canova was the muralist for three notable commissions in New Orleans: the James Robb Mansion in the Garden District, the St. Louis Hotel, and the French Opera House, both in the French Quarter. None of the buildings have survived.

The principal house at Poplar Grove was originally the Banker's Pavilion at the 1884 World's Industrial and Cotton Centennial Exposition in New Orleans. The pavilion was moved from its site in present-day Audubon Park to Poplar Grove, where it was remodeled as a full-time planter's residence.

The center hall at Poplar Grove was created after the house was moved there. Originally, the ladies' and gentlemen's parlors were separated by a wall partition that could be opened to create one large room. Hanging above the English Gothic library table is a contemporary painting by Louisiana artist Jim Blanchard that depicts Poplar Grove as the Banker's Pavilion. The inlaid, horsehair-covered chair is Victorian. Other hall furnishings include the Sheraton settee and Eastlake plant stand, and Renaissance Revival pier mirror on the right. On the left is an armoire from Natchez constructed of tulip poplar flanked by an aesthetic-movement bronze and marble plant stand. Ollie, the family dog, guards the front door from the gallery.

The downriver parlor at Poplar Grove served as a bedroom for owner Ann Wilkinson during her childhood. The walls and ceiling are covered in wallpaper by Bradbury & Bradbury, a firm noted for their hand-printed art wallpapers based on historical antecedents. These wallpapers are copies of designs by Christopher Dresser and William Morris that reflect the oriental influences popular during the aesthetic movement. The upper window sashes consist of sixty small panes of stained glass in a checkerboard pattern. The English ebonized and gilded parlor furniture is characteristic of the aesthetic movement. The wall bracket, another aesthetic design, features ebonized, gilded, and mirrored elements. The sherry glass on the bamboo library stand is from the 1884 New Orleans Exposition. The carved rosewood settee and armchair are American. The chandelier overhead is a bronze gasolier made in New York in 1885 that has since been electrified. The antique Chinese rug is an appropriate complement to the *chinois* influences of the aesthetic pieces throughout the parlor.

In a corner of the men's parlor of Poplar Grove, hanging above a Renaissance Revival American parlor cabinet, is an oil painting by Jane Chauvin, Ann Wilkinson's great-aunt, executed when she was a student of Ellsworth Woodward at Newcomb College in New Orleans.

RIGHT

From the master bedroom, on the left, is a partial view of a mahogany full tester bed. A French gilt mirror hangs above the mantel, on which an assortment of family pictures is displayed, including a photograph of General James Wilkinson, one of the two United States commissioners who formally received the transfer of the Louisiana Territory from France in 1803. Two blue glass vases hold greenery from the garden. A tinted lithograph of Napoleon is reflected in the mirror.

The dining room mantel is one of four matching ones added after the house was moved to Poplar Grove from New Orleans. The Dutch Baroque Revival style chandelier hangs over the dining table, which is covered by an antique Persian serapi rug. The portrait is thought to be Charles Stuart—Bonnie Prince Charlie. The china is English stoneware dating from the period of the house.

RIGHT

Originally a screened porch, this room was enclosed in the 1950s and is currently used as an informal seating area. The painting on the right, done by Clark Hulings in 1970, depicts the sugarcane harvest at Poplar Grove.

The overseer's cottage at Homestead Plantation is a modest building that belies a sophisticated interior put together by current resident Michael Hopping. In the center of the front parlor is an English George IV daybed converted to a sofa. On the left is an Empire mahogany chair that came from De La Ronde Plantation. The adjacent sidetable is late Empire mahogany from the Bancroft Company in Massachusetts. The art consists primarily of Louisiana swamp-scene paintings; the ones on the lower left and right are by Clarence Millet. The mid-left swamp scene is by Knute Heldner. The upper left canvas, an exception to the general theme, is English impressionist. Prominent on the left is a portrait of a Creole gentleman by an unknown artist. On the right is a cypress bracket supporting a blackamoor statuette. The portrait on the lower right is by contemporary Louisiana artist Douglas Bourgeois. The upper right painting is a swamp scene by noted New Orleans artist Alexander Drysdale. The cotton muslin window covering is historically correct, unlike the other furnishings, which would have been found only in a grander house.

Landscape designer Michael Hopping uses this room as his office and studio. On the right is a walnut plantation desk from about 1840. On the desk is an arts-and-crafts oak lamp with a hand-colored Walter Anderson woodblock print on the wall above. A wooden art deco chair is poised at Hopping's drafting desk. On top of the bookcase is a collection of ceramic figurines from Shearwater Pottery designed by Walter Anderson.

RIGHT

The bedroom opens to the studio behind it and to the parlor adjacent. The bed is draped in a *mosquitaire*, which Hopping prizes for its functionality. When the weather is pleasant he likes to open the house up at night, and the *mosquitaire* keeps out mosquitoes while allowing the breeze to waft through. The art on the right is an arrangement of lithographic prints.

MARIETTA'S COTTAGE

This modest cypress-constructed cottage is in the Old Turnerville section of the town of Plaquemine. It is essentially an 1880s shotgun cottage that in 1915 was embellished with craftsman bungalow details—a transformation that the current owner, J. E. Bourgoyne, acknowledges in his description of the house as a "Louisiana bungalow." O'Neal Loupe and Marietta Gelpi Loupe acquired the house in 1915, and Marietta, surviving her husband, lived there until contemporary times. Now, siblings J. E. Bourgoyne and Brenda Bourgoyne Blanchard—two of Marietta's grandchildren—along with J. G. Tyburski, operate the house as a museum exemplifying the small-town way of life that once typified the River Road. The house is a trove of Louisiana mementos and family heirlooms.

The entry to Marietta's cottage is framed by a wisteria-draped arbor that was planted about sixty years ago by Marietta Loupe.

RIGHT

Hanging on the door is Marietta's gardening hat; next to it her kitchen apron hangs on a nail. The doorway opens out to a screened rear porch and the backyard. Marietta and her husband, O'Neal, who earned a living as a carpenter, were typical of the working-class families of Old Turnerville. Both were Catholics, and both were from old Louisiana families. Though their existence was strictly working class, they both were descended from wealthy planter families. Like many planter descendants, theirs was a very different existence from that of their forebears.

This view, at the rear of the house, looks from the kitchen table across to a small bedroom. On the left is a partial view of a kitchen safe purchased in 1915 from Verret's Furniture Store in Plaquemine for $7. In the bedroom is an old iron bed, which J. E. Bourgoyne restored to its original condition. The footboard, which had been cut off in the 1950s in an attempt to create a Hollywood-style bed, then the fashion of the day, had been used as a rose trellis in the rear yard. Also reclaimed from the yard were the original shutters from the house, which, when screens became available in the early twentieth century, had been removed and used to build a pigpen.

GLENDALE PLANTATION

Since 1922, the Lanaux family has owned Glendale Plantation. Through the years the family has steadfastly maintained the principal house even though it no longer serves as a full-time residence.

This view from the dining room to the main parlor at Glendale shows the transitional elements of single-hung sash windows flanking a centered pair of French doors. In a more typical Creole house the two rooms would have been joined by two pairs of French doors, but here the Anglo hierarchy of a central, emphasized entry flanked by Anglo sash windows connects the two rooms.

In a rear bedroom, an antebellum grand-tour copy of an Old Master hangs between two single beds.

RIGHT

This parlor at Glendale is now used as a bedroom. The wooden beam ceiling is a distinguishing characteristic of Creole buildings. Even in later Creole houses, or in more elaborate ones, in which the beams were covered and the ceiling trimmed with classically inspired moldings or frieze work, the Creoles commonly utilized wooden ceilings rather than plaster.

 The full tester bed is a Louisiana Federal–style bed. All the furniture in Glendale came from the Lanaux household at 2023 Esplanade Avenue in New Orleans, which had been in the family since the 1870s or 1880s. The furniture was transferred to Glendale around 1960.

Nottoway is the largest surviving antebellum house on the River Road. One of the most classically detailed, it is the work of Irish-born architect Henry Howard, who was commissioned by John Hampden Randolph, a Virginian of English descent. Conceptually, the house owes nothing discernible to anyone or anything Creole.

The double parlors at Nottoway, referred to as the ballroom, were intended as a grand setting for debutante balls. The Randolph family had seven daughters, five of whom were married in these parlors. The plaster frieze work is by the noted local craftsman Jeremiah Supple, whose trademark was the incorporation of camellia blooms into his designs. The oil painting above the fireplace, painted by James Alexander in 1857, is of a lady, Mary Henshaw. It has no direct connection to Nottoway other than being of the correct period. The chandeliers are original to the house.

Traditionally, the second-floor center hall was used by the family as a parlor, a fact that inspired this current arrangement. The grand center halls in most plantations were used both as corridors of circulation and as rooms. The Louis XIV–style furniture was chosen by Arlin Dease, from St. Francisville, who purchased Nottoway as a speculative venture in 1980 to restore and then resell it. Dease sold it to the current owner, Paul Ramsey, an Australian who has kept it open to the public.

The painting near center on the far wall depicts a setting from a nineteenth-century French novel about two lovers killed at sea.

RIGHT

Arlin Dease in his period re-creation of 1980 selected the early-nineteenth-century musical instruments in this upstairs room. The chair in front of the harp, however, is original to the house. The curtains are contemporary designs based on the descriptions in Cornelia Randolph Murrell's fictional work, *The White Castle of Louisiana*. Murrell, one of Randolph's daughters, loosely based her novel on childhood remembrances from Nottoway.

In the downriver front bedroom, framed by the posts of a full tester bed, is an armoire made in New Orleans by Dutreuil Barjon, Jr. Barjon was a Creole of color who had a shop on Royal Street from 1830 to 1841. The mahogany armoire is in the Empire style.

The mahogany, full **tester** bed in the upriver front bedroom dates from about 1830 and was produced for the New Orleans market in the Empire style. Its design incorporates acanthus leaves and a pineapple motif, symbolizing hospitality. A **trundle** bed beneath can be pulled out when needed to accommodate additional guests. At the foot of the bed is a *lit de repose* (resting bed or day bed) of the same period that also incorporates an acanthus leaf design. The mahogany armoire is mid-nineteenth century.

This fireplace is in the lower downriver parlor of St. Joseph. According to Edmond Simon, the caretaker, the mantel fell to the floor one night in a spectacular crash. The violent noise initially made him suspect the presence of a burglar, but on entering this parlor he discovered the source of the racket. The termite-ridden remains of the mantel have since been stored away.

RIGHT

The grand center hall at St. Joseph, looking out to the rear loggia. St. Joseph Plantation, due to a remodeling in 1858, has many transitional elements reflecting both Creole and Anglo design predilections. The proportions, construction, and roof reflect Creole traditions, while the classical detailing and grand center hall reflect Anglo traditions.

The main parlors at St. Joseph have essentially been unoccupied for some time. Until the fall of 1997, Edmond Simon lived in a caretaker apartment in a small area of the ground floor. While living at St. Joseph, Simon stored these various items of furniture in the parlors. The movie *Grand Isle,* based on Kate Chopin's novel *The Awakening,* was filmed in the house in 1991. The movie company patinated the walls, which had always been whitewashed plaster; grained the woodwork; and put in linoleum flooring designed to resemble a hardwood floor—temporary modifications that all remain.

RIGHT

Looking across the main floor of St. Joseph reveals a cadence of aligned doorways. The hybrid nature of St. Joseph is evident in the lack of French doors and the lack of a hallway between rooms. Both Anglo and Creole predilections are exhibited within a single house.

HOME PLACE PLANTATION

Creole plantation houses usually placed the stairs connecting floors beneath the galleries. When the galleries totally enclosed the house, the stairs were typically at opposing corners, like they originally were at Home Place. Also, because the interior rooms were arranged *en suite,* without internal hallways, the gallery functioned as a corridor of circulation between rooms. Seen from the perspective of how these houses were lived in, the galleries functioned as rooms.

RIGHT

This room originally would have been the main parlor at Home Place, but in the early twentieth century it was used as then-owner Pierre Keller's bedroom. In order to provide better cooling, the ceilings were raised about three feet in a 1904 remodeling orchestrated by Theodore Keller, Pierre Keller's son. This resulted in the rather tenuous proportion of the overmantel, which incorporates a mirror in its design. The wallpaper was put up for the filming of the movie *Convicts,* which was filmed here in the late 1980s. The movie was set in 1902, so all the electrical fixtures were removed prior to filming; since the house is unoccupied, they were never reinstalled.

Originally a second parlor, this room later became the dining room. It was expanded with the addition of a slant-sided bay in the 1904 remodeling by Theodore Keller. A portion of the rear gallery was enclosed in the process. Wallpaper installed for the filming of *Convicts* has partially peeled away to reveal another layer of wallpaper beneath.

RIGHT

In keeping with its Creole tradition, Home Place was a raised single-story house with an above-ground basement that incorporated a wine cellar. The old wine racks have survived and extend floor to ceiling along the downriver wall. The Kellers used the wine cellar as the setting for their annual *boucherie*, when they rendered lard, made cracklings, and so forth.

ASHLAND/BELLE HELENE PLANTATION

Once one of the grandest plantations on the River Road, Ashland was built in 1842 by Duncan Kenner, a prodigal Anglo who was in many ways the Southern myth personified. Planter, statesman, gambler, and horse racer, among other attributions, Duncan Kenner was praised by all who knew him or of him. Unlike many of his fellow Confederates, Kenner's fortunes did not evaporate with the futile war effort. He was worth over a million dollars when he died in 1887.

Shell Chemical Company acquired Ashland in May 1992 from the Hayward family as part of a 102-acre parcel. Shell had no need for the principal house, but not wanting to be seen in the eyes of the community as an unwitting accomplice to Ashland's demise, Shell decided to purchase the house along with the land they needed for plant expansion. Shell put a new roof on Ashland and, in the fall of 1997, repainted the exterior to its original colors—lemon yellow with green shutters and white trim. These steps, along with continued exterior maintenance, guarantee the preservation of the house. There are no specific plans for the restoration of the interiors, since with no specific use in mind, a massive restoration is rather impractical.

This view of the double parlors at Ashland shows the exposed masonry foundations beneath the main floor, which rotted out and had to be removed.

RIGHT

A graceful stair ascends from the rear of the center hall. The outlines of two pieces of art can be seen on the left, telltale reminders of a movie production company's patination of the walls. Seven movies and several music videos have been filmed here, among them *Band of Angels* (1957), *The Beguiled* (1971), *The Autobiography of Miss Jane Pittman* (1974), *The Long, Hot Summer* (1985), and *Fletch Lives* (1989). Ashland's previous owners had not occupied the house on a regular basis since the 1920s, and for about twenty-five years it was completely abandoned. Post–World War II efforts at restoration were not fruitful. Revenue from movie companies was about the only source of income that the grand mansion provided.

The elegant ceiling medallion in the front parlor has survived, though the chandelier that once graced it is long since gone. A bare lightbulb hangs beneath the plaster Greek Revival design of acanthus and shell motifs.

LEFT

The center hall on the second floor features grand Greek Revival doorways opening onto the gallery at either end. This view looks out to the grounds in front of the house. These walls, like those in the stairwell, were patinated for a movie production.

RIGHT

This upstairs bedroom is perhaps the most atrophied of any of the interior spaces at Ashland. An active roof leak prior to the installation of the current roof was the major contributing factor to the decayed condition of this room. Other interior spaces show scars from a fire scene filmed in the house for the movie *Fletch Lives*. The fire got out of control, and before it could be put out, damage was done that has never been repaired.

The armoire in the bedroom of Magnolia Lane is part of a Greek Revival suite of bedroom furniture that dates from the 1860s. The mirrors may have been added later. To the left is a view through the center hall to another bedroom opposite.

RIGHT

The front bedroom is furnished with a Greek Revival suite that dates from the 1860s or 1870s. The wallpaper dates from about 1946. The chandelier came from a house in Pass Christian completely destroyed by Hurricane Camille in 1969. It was found lying in the beach sand and was brought to Magnolia Lane. Three pairs of French doors open this room up to surrounding galleries. For many years, this bedroom was unoccupied—the doors locked and shuttered by resident Grace Naberschnig—because so many people had died in it during the ninety years she lived at Magnolia Lane.

Richard Naberschnig, and his sisters Nancy Parkerson and Elinor Smith, who are descendants of the Quinette family that first purchased the house in 1867, own Magnolia Lane today.

The grand center hall was once divided into two rooms to help accommodate the extended family of fifteen then living in the house. The beaded ceiling boards were installed in a 1915 remodeling. Today the cooling center hall functions as an office and an ancillary space for the adjacent parlors, which are used as bedrooms and a dining room.

ABOVE LEFT
Beside the front door in the center hall, a weathered reproduction of the Persac River Road map of 1858 sits on the floor beneath a photographic portrait of Nancy Parkerson, a Quinette descendant who grew up at Magnolia Lane.

GERMANIA PLANTATION

The principal house at Germania has now been unoccupied for almost twenty years. The roof of the Victorian Eastlake building collapsed in the mid-1990s, and the center hall is now open to the sky. The furniture has been covered over with plastic tarps in an effort to provide some protection from the elements, but if left in this state, it is only a matter of time before building and furniture meet the same fate.

This bedroom is situated in that area of the house where a portion of the roof is still intact, although the collapsed plaster and slivers of skylight between the laths are evidence that the room takes on rainwater. The wooden components of a full tester bed, along with several other pieces of furniture, remain in the room. The room is also filled with books and family heirlooms that have been stored away as best as these marginal conditions allow.

Germania is owned by descendants of John Reuss, one of the wealthiest sugar planters in late-nineteenth-century Louisiana. For reasons that are both complex and enigmatic, the descendants have been unable to maintain the property to a meaningful standard. Many of the outbuildings are in reasonably good condition and could easily be saved. The principal house now exists in one of those brief fragile moments, like a patient with a rapidly weakening pulse. It is conceivable that parts of the principal house could be saved, but only if immediate action is taken.

WHITNEY PLANTATION

The stairs at Whitney are beneath the front and rear galleries, in keeping with the Creole tradition. The dining room was on the ground floor, and service rooms, including a wine cellar, were adjacent to it, but all other living areas were on the second floor. This rear stair, beneath the loggia, brought you into the living spaces at Whitney with drama provided by the elaborate murals that graced the loggia walls.

RIGHT

The rear loggia and main parlor at Whitney were painted with elaborate murals in the mid-nineteenth century when the house was about five decades old. The rear loggia was painted in trompe l'oeil to simulate paneling on the walls around and above the French doors. Between the two doors, beneath a painted arch, a small figure floats above an urn atop a pedestal. There is a distinctively Italianate quality to the loggia murals, which local tradition attributes to Dominique Canova, an Italian immigrant artist from Milan working in New Orleans during the mid-nineteenth century. Canova's surname might actually have been Casanova, and he might have changed it to that of the famous sculptor Antonio Canova as a career-enhancement maneuver. Contemporary examinations of the murals at Whitney and San Francisco plantations have produced the consensus that the murals in both houses were the work of the same artist and in both cases, the local lore credited Canova as the artist. Canova was known to be active in the area. In the late 1830s, he taught art at Jefferson College in Convent. By 1840 he had settled permanently in New Orleans, where he died in 1868.

The main parlor at Whitney is a grand space with hand-painted murals adorning the ceiling and door panels. The mantels are of the Creole wrap-around type, with the chimney flues wrapped in a Creole Federal-style over-mantel. On the ceiling above the mantel are the elaborately painted initials MH for Marcellin Haydel, the owner of the house when these murals were executed. White-plastered walls trimmed in ochre constitute a classic Creole color scheme.

The downriver parlor at Whitney has a prominent Creole mantel with Federal details. The floor is of wide cypress boards. The aqua walls, though probably not the original color, impart a quiet melancholy to the empty room.

RIGHT
A detail of the hand-painted ceiling medallion in the main parlor at Whitney. A central rosette is encircled first by a wreath of flowers, then by a classically inspired trompe l'oeil roundel with filigreed axial elements, and finally by a band of ivy.

    A Grand Illusion All.

THE AMBIENCE OF THE COUNTRYSIDE

CHAPTER THREE

"A triangular Greek pediment rose to give the effect of additional height. At the back, almost out of sight, extended the 'street,' a pathway with sets of brick cottages in close rows—the negro quarters. . . . Framing it all was the flaring vegetation of near tropic Louisiana: explosions of foliage; bushes startling in size and coloration; hedges of roses, soft in their waves of pink; the bristling jaggedness of the Spanish daggers, protecting their inner blossomings of high, cool white; and the camellias, trees of red flowers that hung in every direction. Lines of live oaks, each a hill of green leaves, reached from the houses to the river, while other growths half-buried the buildings in borders and tangled draperies across the front. A mile or so away settled the shifting blue haze of the forests. At the three sides of the clearing a sea of the staple crop lapped its way—endless processions of the sugar cane, tasseled tops waving under the light currents of air, or the low files of gray-white cotton bolls. This land seemed to swell and break into bloom."

HARNETT KANE

Plantation Parade: The Grand Manner in Louisiana,

1945

The dominant impression of plantation life was that of the surrounding countryside. The built environment, by comparison, could be likened to a ship at sea—tiny and isolated amid an intimidating vastness. When in the early eighteenth century the first European settlers arrived intent on carving up the wilderness and establishing an agrarian colony, they were confronted by the sinuous river, marshy back swamps, and virgin forests thinly populated by villages of Native Americans. The land was cleared to make way for fields, and a levee system with a rutted road at its base gradually evolved in patchwork fashion. As houses were built, their grandeur was complemented by formal gardens and *allées* of trees framing views to the river. Vegetable and herb gardens were planted, and animals were raised for food. Fields, gardens, forests, swamps, and, most importantly, the river placed an expansive verdant framework around life on the plantation.

An old wagon abandoned on the grounds of Home Place by a movie production company has since been used as a hay trough for feeding livestock—a metaphor for much of the countryside of the River Road.

RIGHT

A detail of the lower trunk of one of the twenty-eight gnarled oaks at Oak Alley Plantation. These oaks were planted in the early eighteenth century by a French colonist whose identity has been lost to history; they are now about 250 years old. They have an average life expectancy of about 400 years. The live oak, perhaps because of its scale and its ability to transform the character of open space, is the most dominant natural feature of the River Road.

PREVIOUS

Behind the principal house at Home Place is a stand of mature oaks planted when the house was first built. Their heavy arching limbs once shaded a kitchen building and other outbuildings that have since been lost to time. In the right foreground is a shallow well once used as a source of nonpotable water for the gardens and livestock. Beyond this gnarly canopy, the fields begin.

An iris blooms in the midst of a cypress swamp.

RIGHT

The geographic pattern of the River Road consists of high ground along the natural levee near the river, followed by a flood plain of silted-up land that gradually dissolves into watery cypress swamps. This swamp is behind the cane fields in the Gramercy-Lutcher area on the east bank. Swamps formed the back geographic boundary to the River Road landscape and, like the arable land, was highly exploitable, for it was there that the giant cypress trees grew that were felled to build the plantation houses and the city of New Orleans. Ultimately, the virgin swamp-forests were completely logged and the trees here represent new growth that is less than one hundred years old.

These cypress boards of *pieux* fencing have, over time, assumed a rich organic patina. *Pieux* fencing, favored by the Creoles, has a natural organic quality and blends readily with its verdant surroundings.

On the grounds of Manresa Retreat House, in Convent on the east bank, this oak *allée* forms a tranquil, meditative arcade between the River Road and the levee.

The cast-iron balusters at Nottoway Plantation are silhouetted by light filtered through the leaves and moss of the surrounding live oak trees. Spanish moss dripping from the arching limbs of live oaks became the stereotypical visual embodiment of the antebellum South.

RIGHT

A sympathetic blend of the old and the new. A window from an old slave cabin at Homestead Plantation frames a view to a contemporary conservatory built in 1996. Michael Hopping designed the conservatory for John and Cindy Hill, who reside in the original Homestead Plantation principal house. The conservatory is used to grow orchids and tropical plants and for wintering small potted plants.

These steps are the only remnant of a kitchen building that had been appended to the principal house at Home Place in the early twentieth century. This kitchen was built at half height, between the ground floor and upper floor, and last functioned as a kitchen in the 1930s. It collapsed in about 1992. A heavy oak limb in the background echoes the descent of the steps.

RIGHT
An inviting Louisiana ladderback chair sits on the front gallery at Desiré Plantation. Galleries on plantation residences offered an ideal spot to look out to the verdant surroundings, particularly in the early mornings and late afternoons when the heat was less stifling.

Unfolding leaf buds of a *fatsia japonica*.

LEFT
Hand-molded Italian terra-cotta pots hold wire topiaries.

Michael Hopping, a landscape designer who resides in the overseer's cottage at Homestead Plantation, has fashioned a small garden evocative of nineteenth-century Louisiana cottage gardens to complement his modest house. The plants, however, differ from historical examples. The garden pavilion is a new addition, completed in the spring of 1998. The focal point of the garden is the old privy from Homestead Plantation, which is now used as a gardener's shed. It was moved from behind the principal house upriver to the garden. A pre-1850 structure, it is built of hand-hewn cypress held together with wooden pegs. As Michael Hopping proudly proclaims, "It's a three-holer."

The metal Parisian patio chairs in the pavilion are complemented by steamship deck chairs. The diamond boxwood hedge surrounding the privy contains an herb garden. This type of diamond motif is pervasive in Louisiana antiquities.

A board-and-batten shutter and exposed water pipes on the ground floor of the principal house at Whitney Plantation have become unwitting trellises for a vine.

LEFT
The backlight of early morning delineates the intricate veining of large elephant ear leaves at L'Hermitage Plantation.

The verdant subtropical foliage in rain-soaked south Louisiana can encroach menacingly when nature is left to run its course. A small building near the principal house at Bocage Plantation has been overcome by foliage; only the rusty roof is visible from the air. The forests and swamps become impenetrable at the height of summer foliation.

Behind Destrehan Plantation, on the verge of the swamp, twin smokestacks from an abandoned oil refinery poke through the forest that has reclaimed the site. Destrehan had been the site of an oil refinery since 1914, first as Mexican Petroleum Company and finally as American Oil Company, which closed down the refinery in 1959. Like the plantations before them, oil refineries make for intriguing ruins.

The traditional harvesting method first cuts the cane at the base of the stalk and then consolidates four cane rows into two, which are called "heap rows." The cut cane is then burned in the field to remove all the leaves so that only the stalk remains. The charred stalks are then carted to the mill for processing into raw sugar.

A close view shows heap rows of cane as the fire line makes its way across the field.

LEFT

A new type of harvester, referred to as a chopper harvester, harvests this field of cane. This technology, which has been available for about five years, allows harvesting without burning the cane. Though it produces dramatic atmospheric effects, the fall cane burning is a major source of air pollution.

The cane harvest is the annual fall event of the River Road and the culmination of an agrarian cycle. Beginning in early October and culminating no later than December, the harvest is a race against the frost of winter. Because Louisiana is only subtropical and cane is a tropical plant, the harvest and subsequent protection of the cane roots during the winter months is an unforgiving process.

In this panoramic view, the foreground field is being burned. Fields of mature cane in the background await harvest. Billowy clouds of smoke envelop the River Road—an eerie signal that the cane harvest has begun.

Following harvest, the cane roots are protected from frost during the winter months; the following spring, a new cane crop is grown from the old roots. After three or four years, the cane roots must be plowed under and the fields are left idle for a year to prevent diminished yields.

In these fields, preparations are being made for the land to lay idle for a year, after which it will be replanted and the cycle will begin anew.

A closer view shows a flock of seagulls from the Gulf of Mexico trailing the tractor. Seagulls range far inland during the winter months.

Behind the closed shutter of the abandoned *Maison de Reprise* at Laura Plantation is a bird's nest, an incidental and accidental mingling of nature with the man-made on the River Road.

RIGHT

At Felicity Plantation, just upriver from the site of the gardens of Valcour Aime, peacocks are raised as living adornments to the principal house, which Valcour Aime had originally built for his daughter Felicité. Their flight from limb to limb on the giant oaks in front of Felicity and the showy mating spectacle put on by the male birds are entrancing. Perhaps the exotic spirit of the legendary Valcour Aime is being carried on. Stan Waguespack, who raises the peacocks, remembers as a very young boy standing on the front gallery of Felicity with his grandmother and watching helplessly as Valcour Aime's abandoned plantation house next door burned to the ground.

The many crawfish holes that dot the muddy river silt of plantation sites are as common as ants at a picnic. Prior to federal levee control, when each plantation owner maintained his own levee, crevasses were common during the spring high-water season. Crawfish holes that had weakened the levee were frequently the source of blame for the crevasses. The venerable crawfish, and former levee nemesis, has become a staple of the Louisiana diet.

Elmwood Plantation was near the Huey P. Long Bridge in Harahan, a suburb of New Orleans. In contemporary local usage, Elmwood is known as a shopping center and office park, but these contemporary Elmwoods are the namesakes of the plantation that once occupied this site.

The 1938 WPA *New Orleans Guide* described a much different Elmwood than these photographs document: "Left about 300 yards is *Elmwood*, an antebellum mansion standing near the foot of the levee. The thick walls and heavy columns of this house suggest a frontier stronghold, an impression deepened by barred windows and narrow gun slots which pierce the east wall of the ground floor. There is not an elm on or near the plantation, but thirty-two magnificent oaks."

In the 1940s, the abandoned Elmwood was gutted by fire. A restaurant was fashioned from the portion that survived. It operated into the 1970s, when another fire left only these ruins of the masonry foundation, which nature is slowly reclaiming. Lush, resilient undergrowth is on the verge of swallowing the basement story, and resurrection ferns sprout from its walls. As grand and as solid as the plantation houses were, the natural environment of south Louisiana always seemed more powerful. The verdant foliage and the capricious river were constant reminders that, in the end, nature would pervade.

In 1997, when these photographs were taken, the site was being offered for sale. The following year, the ruins were bulldozed and site improvements commenced for "Elmwood Plantation Estates," a subdivision of twenty-six homesites offering yet another reference to the now-vanished Elmwood.

Valcour Aime was one of the most prominent Creole planters in Louisiana. After extensively remodeling his plantation house between 1832 and 1836, Aime began the construction in 1843 of what he termed a *jardin anglais,* an English Park. Incorporating whimsical architectural features within an artificial wilderness, it is evocative of the gardens of the European nobility now commonly referred to as folly gardens, such as Ermenonville near Paris.

Aime enlisted the assistance of Joseph Mueller, from Jardin des Plantes, a botanical garden and museum in Paris, to assist in the creation of his fanciful garden. Slaves carved "rivulets" that were fed by a waterfall "cascade." The rivulets flowed into a reflecting pond featuring an island overlook fashioned like a stone fortification—the "fort." Nearby, a large mound was constructed, crowned by a Chinese pagoda, with a grotto beneath in which Aime went to pray. Local legend has it that exotic animals, including even kangaroos, roamed the *petit bois,* or small woods. Whereas this is likely to have been the case, it stretches credulity that animals as exotic as kangaroos were among them. Though local lore may have embellished its exoticness, Aime's garden was unique to the River Road. While neighboring planters were content with their formal parterre gardens and *allées* of planted trees, Aime clearly desired something more contemporary and adventuresome.

Today Aime's whimsical garden, known colloquially as "Le Petit Versailles," lies in ruin—a dense, almost impenetrable thicket flanked by River Road cane fields on two sides. A caretaker owner purchased it to thwart the plans of others who saw it as a potential site for suburban development. The remnants of this garden and the family tomb in St. James Cemetery are the only physical remnants of the legacy of Valcour Aime. His mansion, which had been abandoned by the early twentieth century, burned to the ground in the 1920s. A contemporary house now occupies the site.

In the photo above, the only surving "Roman" bridge spans a rivulet.

The ruins of the grotto. No trace remains of the Chinese pagoda that once crowned it.

RIGHT
The remains of the reflecting pond with its island overlook. Ruins of the fort are still visible on the island.

THE CULTURAL LANDSCAPE

"A purely natural landscape is one which has never been occupied by man. An area which is unified upon the basis of the way in which man has used and transformed the natural landscape is a cultural landscape."

EDNA SCOFIELD

from an article defining house types within a cultural geography,

1936

In truth, every aspect of the plantation and the balance of the built environment ancillary to it is an evocation of the culture of the planters. Certain of these elements speak so powerfully and poignantly to the culture of a people that they overshadow whatever else they may be about. The cultural collisions and collusions among the Anglos and the Creoles became a powerful force along the River Road. An equally significant cultural tension existed between people of African and European descent. The German peasants recruited by John Law in the early days of the colony made an enduring contribution to the local culture. The omnipresent Catholic church also had a lasting influence. One of the most compelling characteristics of the New World is the way in which diverse cultures that had limited opportunity to intermingle in the Old World would mix together in a hybrid fashion. The River Road was a mixing bowl that ultimately produced a unique cultural landscape.

The portrait of a postbellum planter, Adam Barthelemy Jones, the adopted son of Barthelemy Haydel. Jones was born in 1867 and died in 1936. He lived the entirety of his life on the Haydel-Jones plantation and farmed cane as his father before him had done. The plantation is still owned by his descendants.

RIGHT

An old iron cross leans precariously against a brick tomb in St. James Cemetery. It bears the name of Cleveland Lear, an infant born in 1914 who lived only to the age of one and a half years. Infant mortality remained high in rural Louisiana, since medical treatment was neither as available nor as advanced as it was in urban areas.

Louisiana ducks roasting in the open hearth at Destrehan plantation. Sweet potatoes bake in the hot embers below the fire. The Creoles were known for their rich culinary tradition, which blended French traditions with New World ingredients and new culinary traditions assimilated from the West Indies and Africa.

An annual Christmas banquet is held at Laura Plantation. Lit by candlelight, it is a prelude to the lighting of a Christmas bonfire by the levee. Levee bonfires are an old tradition on the River Road, particularly in St. James Parish.

In early December, the Festival of the Bonfires is held in the Gramercy-Lutcher area as an official beginning to the Christmas Eve ritual of lighting bonfires on the levee. During the weekend festival, bonfire Christmas ornaments and other holiday items are sold on the River Road. Later in the evening, a single bonfire is lit, harbinger of the multitude of bonfires that will follow on Christmas Eve.

LEFT
A bonfire at the Laura Christmas celebration is executed in the traditional manner of St. James Parish—a pyramidal arrangement of outer logs is filled in with additional logs in the center. This bonfire construction is similar to the winter and summer solstice bonfires that are a tradition in parts of Europe, descended from the Celtic religious leaders, the Druids. Bonfires are an old tradition at Laura. A surviving 1871 photograph shows members of the Locoul family gathered around a bonfire.

On Christmas Eve, at seven sharp, all the bonfires that line the levee for several miles are lit. It is believed that the European practice of solstice bonfires is the basis of the local tradition, with the winter solstice date shifted to Christmas Eve. The River Road bonfire tradition has been documented as far back as the nineteenth century. In Cajun oral tradition, the bonfires light the way for "Papa Noel, " their version of Santa Claus. Though popular and endearing, this is not the likely origin, because the bonfire tradition predates Papa Noel. In rural south Louisiana, gifts were traditionally exchanged among Cajun and Creole families on New Year's Day and were followed by visits to the homes of friends and relatives. On Christmas Eve, a *réveillon* (festive celebration) followed midnight mass, and candy and trinkets were exchanged on Christmas Day. Papa Noel is a more recent innovation that attempts to reconcile and assimilate Cajun and Creole celebrations with those of mainstream America.

Above the altar at St. Gabriel Catholic Church, the Sacred Heart of Jesus symbolizes Christ's suffering and self-sacrifice. The Sacred Heart is hand-painted on burlap; it was executed as part of the late-nineteenth-century Gothic remodeling of the old church.

Beneath the remodeling are the structural bones of a much older building. St. Gabriel was built in the 1770s as a church for Acadians who were being settled in the area to thwart further southerly migration of the English. It originally had French casement windows with segmental arches, a broken-pitch roof supported by a Norman truss, and galleries across the front and sides of the structure.

A new church was built on this site in the 1950s behind the old one. St. Gabriel is the only extant church of this type in Louisiana and it is believed to be the oldest church building in the Louisiana Purchase territory. The Catholic tradition in Louisiana is as old as the settlement itself; and the Church, in keeping with Latin tradition, is an integral part of the civic order.

THE CULTURAL LANDSCAPE

Behind the main altar of St. Michael's Catholic Church in Convent is a grotto inspired by its French name-sake, Our Lady of Lourdes. Built in 1876 as an addition to the church of 1833, it is constructed of bagasse clinkers, hard pieces of charred bagasse. (Bagasse is a by-product of sugar crystallization—the pulpy remnant of cane stalks that have had their juice extracted—that is ordinarily burned to fire the boilers at the mill.) Parishioners come to the grotto to light votive candles and offer their prayers.

This icon of the Blessed Mother is in the front garden of Desiré Plantation, nestled between the roots of a live oak. It was a gift from the great-granddaughter of Philippe Desiré LeBlanc, the plantation's namesake, to the current owners. All along the River Road, in gardens and sometimes in elaborately conceived altars and grottoes, are statuettes of the Blessed Mother. Typically, they are not antique, nor are they made of fine materials—most are concrete. They are a simple expression of faith and an icon of the Catholicism that is so pervasive and enduring in the region.

RIGHT

The main sanctuary of St. Michael's Catholic Church in Convent is one of the most impressive religious spaces on the River Road. The handsome masonry structure, which dates from 1833, was built in the Gothic Revival style. St. Michael's was founded so that east bank residents would not have to cross the river to St. James' Church to attend mass. With its richly carved woodwork and highly elaborated Gothic detailing, St. Michael's is evocative of the fine old churches common to small towns throughout Europe.

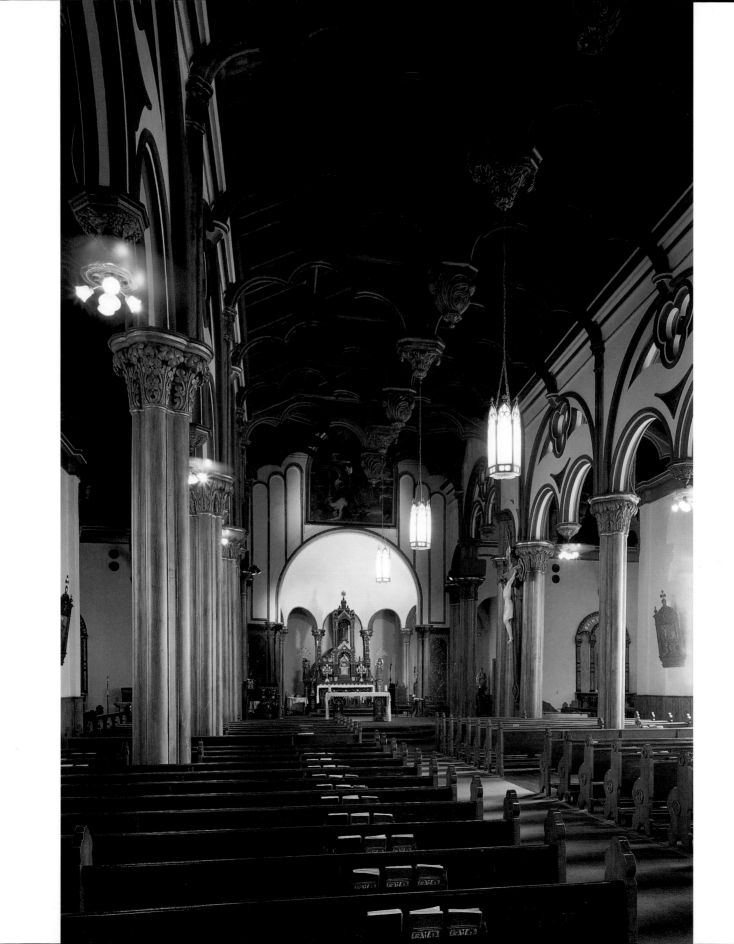

Just above the community of White Castle, on the west bank, is the black settlement of Dorseyville. At the heart of Dorseyville is St. John Baptist Church, founded in 1868 by the Reverend Bazil Dorsey, after whom the community is named. Dorseyville was created by freed slaves from nearby plantations who built their homes around Dorsey's church. This church building is essentially vernacular, with restrained Gothic details. It was placed on the National Register in 1994.

In the main sanctuary, above the altar, are photographs of the pastors of St. John Baptist Church, beginning with the church's founder, Rev. Dorsey. Next to Dorsey is the pastor who succeeded him in 1900, Rev. Washington. There have been only five pastors at St. John Baptist since its founding over 130 years ago.

Behind the pulpit and out of view is the baptismal pool, accessible through a trap door. Before this pool was added in the 1920s, baptisms were conducted in the Mississippi River.

St. John Baptist Church is a typical example of how black churches served as foundations of community and civic involvement.

On the west bank in St. Charles Parish, just above the community of Hahnville, in the front yard of the Zeringue house, is a small vegetable stand that the family runs in the spring and summer months. All the vegetables are grown in a small garden behind the main house. The Zeringues are descendants of German Coast settlers. The German Coast was first settled by Swiss and German peasants recruited by the French government to help establish its agrarian colony in Louisiana, and the settlers were given very modest land grants, where they raised livestock and maintained small farms. The fruits of their labors were largely devoted to the sustenance of the urban population downriver in New Orleans. The roadside stands along the River Road were the logical descendants of German Coast agriculture, but very few remain today. The River Road is no longer a major thoroughfare, and supermarkets in the larger towns are readily accessible to rural residents. However, those few remaining stands, like the Zeringues, are supported by a loyal following who prefer homegrown fruits and vegetables.

The St. Joseph P & M Store is the only plantation store on the River Road between New Orleans and Baton Rouge still in operation. Several other plantation store buildings remain standing, but they have long since shut their doors. The P & M in the store's name stands for "planting" and "manufacturing," referring to the planting of cane and the manufacture of sugar. Most plantations are now set up as family corporations, and the "P & M" appellation is quite common. The St. Joseph store dates from the early 1870s. Historically, the wife of the overseer of the plantation always ran the store. The range of merchandise has been supplemented in recent years by tourist items and River Road memorabilia in an effort to keep the store financially viable.

LEFT

Set back only a few feet from the River Road is the abandoned plantation store at Whitney. Plantation stores, sometimes referred to as commissaries, were a fixture on major plantations in the postbellum era. The typical plantation workforce included many families, all of whom lived on the plantation. Given the relatively remote location and the immobility of the workers, plantation owners provided the means of securing provisions through a plantation store. Many sharecroppers and farm laborers were paid in "plantation currency," essentially notes that could be redeemed for merchandise only at the store.

ABOVE LEFT

The scale on the left, used for weighing beans and meats, is of 1970s vintage. The string box above was used to dispense string to tie up wrapped bundles of merchandise. Behind the counter are shelves of packaged merchandise.

ABOVE RIGHT

The "Lance" canister, originally used for crackers, now holds chewing gum. The ledger in the foreground is still used to record purchases for house accounts.

RIGHT

This cash register dates from about 1940. It was damaged in a burglary in the late 1980s and has not been used since.

"Famille Valcour Aime" identifies the family tomb of the famed River Road planter known as the Louis XIV of Louisiana. Valcour Aime's remains have since been relocated from St. James Cemetery to St. Louis Cemetery No. 1 in New Orleans. St. James Cemetery, pressed tightly between the River Road and the levee, dates from the founding of the original church at this site in 1770. Many tombs have been lost to the river over time. The Valcour Aime family tomb now rests at the very base of the levee.

RIGHT

Near the back of The Ascension of Our Lord Cemetery in Donaldsonville, the massive, classically detailed Landry tomb towers above all the others in the cemetery. The design is attributed to New Orleans architect James Dakin.

St. John the Baptist Cemetery, in the town of Edgard, on the west bank, was laid out in 1770. Levee construction in 1881 resulted in the loss of many gravesites when they were washed into the river. The inscriptions on this brick tomb, marked "J. Anatole Perret," are written in French; the cemeteries along the River Road are a vestige of a time when English was very much a secondary language in the area. A cross and the tomb's nameplate lie broken at the base.

RIGHT
A detail of an iron gate leading to a brick tomb marked "L. Fossier." Resurrection ferns sprout from the masonry of the old tomb.

Life—and death—continues along the River Road. Wilting flowers from a recent burial at St. James Cemetery in the spring of 1997.

RIGHT

Holy Rosary Cemetery, a Catholic cemetery whose church has since moved, presents one of the most poetic juxtapositions along the River Road. The small cemetery, just above the community of Hahnville in St. Charles Parish, is completely surrounded by the Taft-Carbide petrochemical plant. The stone-carved crucifix is the most significant icon at Holy Rosary. It is framed, enigmatically, by chemical tanks and exhaust stacks in the background.

The bridge of an oil tanker looms above the crest of the levee at St. James Cemetery. A modern docking facility on the batture adjacent to the cemetery places eighteenth-century gravesites in the immediate proximity of industry. In the middle ground is the tomb of the Valcour Aime family, one of the most celebrated Creole planter families of the River Road.

AFTERWORD

ARCHITECTURE IS AS UNDENIABLY MORTAL AS THE humans who build it. The role of the preservationist is merely to thwart an untimely demise. We deny our own mortality by going to extraordinary lengths to prolong human longevity, but we tend to be far more ambivalent with our architecture. In fact, the willingness to tear down almost anything we have built has been a hallmark of American culture—a predilection that has only recently been subjected to serious reevaluation.

America is about progress and migration, entrepreneurship and the economic exploitation of fertile landscapes. It is also about invention and innovation, hybridization and assimilation. Perhaps most significantly, however, America is about freedom, including the freedom to do whatever one wants with one's property. America is, therefore, less occupied with tradition, heritage, stewardship, and civic duty than many other cultures, including those from which we have directly descended. Though America is a world power economically and militarily, culturally it is merely postcolonial. America is still finding itself, gradually and sometimes painfully; it is becoming a more mature and stable place of human habitation—the cultural equivalent of an adolescent, a brash and prodigal one at that.

Along Louisiana's River Road are scattered some of the most compelling vestiges of our exotic past. Though today we readily recognize the significance of this architecture, we are somewhat baffled by what to do with it. In far too many cases, there is no longer a logical economic reason for this architecture to exist. The plantation houses—built by some of the richest families in America and positioned directly on America's most strategic corridor of transportation, the Mississippi River—have become the victims of a reversal of fortune. The cane farmers of today are not as affluent as their forebears. Other sorts of individuals

LEFT *Canals cut for logging valuable cypress trees have left a striking graphic pattern in the wetland swamp landscape. Logging, oil drilling, and even recreational craft have placed considerable environmental stress on this fragile ecosystem.*

RIGHT *Agriculture and industry coexist. In the middle of the cane fields is an access and service area for an oil pipeline. This juxtaposition of competing land use has come to define the River Road in the latter half of the twentieth century.*

who might be wealthy enough to restore and maintain a plantation house typically desire an address with a level of prestige commensurate with the quality and prestige of the architecture, and the River Road does not always offer that. Virtually no one, regardless of means, wants to live next door to a petrochemical plant. Other logical alternative uses, such as bed and breakfast accommodations, or academic and/or corporate retreats, are also thwarted by the close proximity of industry. A local preservationist described the problem quite succinctly when he told me, "You know, one of the big problems is that the River Road is just not a fashionable place to be."

The petrochemical industry cannot be cast without qualification as the villain in all this. In many cases, this industry represents the only economic power base with the means and the civic obligation to help preserve the historic architecture of the River Road. Those who might assert that the petrochemical industry is the sole threat to the region's historic architecture need to reconcile a certain amount of history to validate their assertion.

The history of the antebellum architecture of the River Road can be characterized as having four distinct periods. The architecture built by the planters had its first and most formidable life in the antebellum period, which commenced with European settlement and terminated with the Civil War. It was during this period that most of the great houses were built and served their initial purpose as grand, showy residences and seats of business for the affluent planter families. Reconstruction brought with it the second period in the life of the plantation house, which I term postbellum utilitarianism. In the hard times of Reconstruction, the solidly built antebellum houses continued to provide shelter to the planters, whose diminished resources fostered a certain enforced gratitude for the presence of substantial and durable shelter. As plantations were bought and sold, so were the principal houses. Over time, however,

The worker cabins at Poplar Grove are currently abandoned and overgrown. Some of the cabins were lived in up until 1996. These double cabins were never occupied by slaves since they were built in the 1870s to accommodate black worker families in the postbellum era. The current owner has proposed plans for an industrial park to be built on this site; but as of this writing the controversial plans have not been approved. The fate of the cabins hangs in the balance.

AFTERWORD

ABOVE AND LEFT *Two textbook examples of the juxtaposition of historic architecture with petrochemical facilities can be observed in these views of Ashland/Belle Helene in Geismar and San Francisco in Garyville. In both cases, the petrochemical companies in proximity have played a significant role in financing and preserving their historical neighbors. Significantly, at both sites the preservation of landscaping and open space around the historic structures has thwarted visual encroachment by the petrochemical presence. The pedestrian experience on the grounds of the historic sites and the vistas from the houses to the immediate environment is isolated from the presence of the petrochemical industry nearby.*

RIGHT *At Triad Nitrogen, just below the town of Donaldsonville, the commendable preservation of an historic building for use as a plant office is compromised by the lack of visual isolation from the plant itself. More thoughtful siting of the industrial structures coupled with an appropriate landscaping program, and a more generous provision for open space around the historic site, could have alleviated this clashing juxtaposition of old and new.*

The site of Elmwood Plantation is now occupied by suburban industrial parks and warehousing facilities. Only the ruins of Elmwood remain; the abandoned and derelict principal house burned in the 1940s. Since these photos were taken in 1997, the site has been cleared to make way for a residential subdivision.

RIGHT *The petrochemical industry is a latecomer in the competition for the planter's agricultural land. In Bywater, a nineteenth-century New Orleans neighborhood, the Lombard House, in the upper center of the frame, is a surviving Creole plantation principal house. Surrounding it is a mix of later residential and light industrial buildings. The urban and suburban growth of New Orleans has claimed many plantations, including the plantation of Etienne de Boré, who first successfully granulated sugar in Louisiana. Audubon Park in uptown New Orleans now occupies the site of the de Boré plantation.*

the grand houses began to deteriorate seriously. Floods and major cane crop failures in the 1920s severely compromised resources needed to keep up what were even then, in some cases, century-old buildings. By the Great Depression, many plantation houses were abandoned, derelict, and on the verge of collapse. Postbellum utilitarianism was coming to an end due to the lack of continued economic practicality. A brief and transitional period—the rehabilitated country estate—supplanted postbellum utilitarianism. In this period, beginning in the late 1930s, an altogether different class of individuals was beginning to look to the historic architecture of the River Road

for residential purposes. After a century of existence, the merely old becomes historic and is perceived as being far more meaningful than the new—provided it can be adequately updated to reflect the needs of a more endowed socioeconomic class. During the era of the rehabilitated country estate, upper-middle-class and wealthy individuals came to view the River Road's historic architecture as a suitable setting from which to craft weekend retreats or country estates. It was during this period that Matilda Gray purchased and remodeled Evergreen; George Crozat saved Houmas House; his sister Anita Crozat Kohlsdorf and her husband brought Bocage back from the brink; and the

Maintenance of the historic architecture of the River Road is a continual, unrelenting chore. Here at Evergreen, just above
Edgard, the graceful, arching stairs of the principal house are being replaced for the second time since the primary restoration of the house
in the 1940s. This time the curved stringers are being constructed of metal in an effort to reduce the frequency of an expensive and
time-consuming endeavor.

Stewarts came to the salvation of Oak Alley after a previous owner had gone bankrupt. These are only some of the most prominent examples of those individuals who rescued River Road plantation architecture at a critical juncture in its lifespan. All these new owners had at least three things in common: They were not River Road cane-planting families; they had the necessary resources and sophistication to save the historic buildings they purchased; and they all used their rehabilitated architecture as either weekend country estates or retirement compounds. The period of the rehabilitated country estate failed to achieve critical mass, however, for several reasons—the expense of rehabilitation and encroachment by the emerging petrochemical industry were prominent among them. But this era did form a key transition to the present, the period of contemporary preservation. At the national level, the economic and cultural significance of historic architecture has finally reached a critical level of awareness. Cultural tourism has emerged as an economic force and a source of employment, and money can be made by offering the experience of plantation architecture to a public eagerly seeking a viable connection to its past. The myth of the Southern planter and the cultural connections between south Louisiana and the Caribbean are more than suitable fodder. In the contemporary period, the primary impetus for the preservation of the historic architecture of the River Road is embedded in the societal recognition that we need to preserve our historic architecture because it is the right thing to do, and this notion is buttressed by the economic viability of cultural tourism.

If one accepts my premise of four dominant periods in the history of River Road architecture, determining which eras have been the most destructive and which the most constructive to the region's historic architecture is a rather straightforward matter. It was the last years of postbellum utilitarianism, when the houses were old and cane planting was becoming less lucrative, combined with the emergence of the petrochemical industry as a viable alternative to cane farming, that saw the loss of so much historic architecture. It was also during this period that the levee system was placed under federal control and expanded. In many cases, historic architecture was readily sacrificed for flood protection. The age and condition of the historic buildings, the inadequate financial means of their owners, the need for River frontage by an emergent petrochemical industry, and the need to radically reengineer the levee all spelled trouble. The 1920s and 1930s were the nadir of the historic architecture of the River Road, and the petrochemical industry was only one contributing factor.

Plantation complexes were falling to rack and ruin long before the petrochemical industry ever arrived on the scene. Since the petrochemical industry has established itself on the River Road, its record has been a mixed bag. Some companies, the more enlightened ones, have played an important role in helping preserve historic architecture. Other companies have torn down historic buildings on their property in the dead of night in order to avoid the obligation of maintaining or restoring them. Regardless of corporate responsibility or the lack thereof, there is no disputing the fact that the immediate proximity of industry, virtually any industry, to historic residential architecture makes adaptive reuse more difficult. The only real solution is regional planning that sets a clear public priority regarding land use and establishes meaningful criteria for avoiding, or at least mitigating, incompatible competitive land uses.

Whereas it is a grand testament to tradition and commitment that some River Road families still own their ancestral homes, this situation is fraught with more complexity than it may seem. The plantation sites, and whatever architecture remains upon them,

TOP *Petrochemical plants are not the only industrial apparitions along the River Road. The Zen-Noh Grain Company, incorporating an intricate array of industrial projections, is actually an agricultural facility. Owned by a Japanese corporation, the firm stores and then custom mixes a variety of grains from the Midwest prior to exportation to international markets.*

The interior of the ground floor of the Maison de Reprise at Laura Plantation is indicative of the typical condition of abandoned plantation buildings on the River Road. The principal house at Laura was in similar condition before its current restoration was commenced. Fortunately, the notion that buildings in this state are too far gone to be restored is no longer the predominant view. Though it is expensive and laborious, modern techniques in architectural restoration can readily save structures such as the Maison.

are only a small, and typically economically meaningless, component of a much bigger whole —a functioning, family-owned cane farm. In Louisiana, there is embedded within the civil code an old and dying vestige of the Code Napoleon—forced heirship. Historically, under state law, you were obliged to leave at least one-half of your total assets to your children, equally divided. Over time, this situation tended to manifest itself in the form of scores of relatives, from siblings to distant cousins who may barely know each other, all jointly owning a small piece of an agricultural enterprise. In most cases, a corporation was established to run the agribusiness with a board consisting of relatives, all of whom hold shares. Today some corporations have over one hundred shareholders. The primary function of the corporation is to run a cane business profitably, but this same bunch of relatives is also encumbered with the task of caring for and deciding the ultimate fate of the historic architecture belonging to the corporation. Often, the old plantation house is a white elephant—unneeded and impractical as a contemporary residence. It can be a maintenance nightmare that if cared for adequately, would severely curtail the profitability of the corporation; it is also awkward, as well as emotionally disturbing, to sell it off. And these are just the obvious problems. Many corporate heads of cane enterprises will tell you that when contentious issues arise, just getting all the relatives to be civil to one another, let alone agreeing on anything, can be quite a chore. Stewardship of a grand architectural relic under these circumstances can be most tenuous. Further, it is one thing to have respect and appreciation for a grand vestige of one's past. It is quite another to have the means and the architectural knowledge needed to ensure preservation and adaptive, profitable reuse of it.

It is obvious to even the most casual of observers that more can and should be done to ensure that the historic architecture of the River Road is preserved. It should also be obvious that the loss of historic architecture is not the result of any single cause, but is a much more complex problem. Ultimately, the task of historic preservation is as simple to define as it is difficult to achieve—for historic architecture to be preserved, there must be an economic reason for it to continue to exist. My personal viewpoint on the complex melange that defines the contemporary River Road landscape is that the dynamic of land use is at a critical crossroads. I see an uncertain future punctuated by hope and fear. I am grateful for the opportunity to have witnessed and chronicled this place at this time; but above all else, I hope that I have made a meaningful difference. If nothing else, I would hope for this alone: In response to all those individuals who might say, "The River Road is lost. It was once filled with the monuments of our past, and the embodiment of all that we accomplished here, and now it is gone. There is nothing left to save." Yes, I will concede that far more than I want to think about has been lost to the ravages of time, but I beg to differ that all has been lost. I rest my case within these pages. This is my testament—the chronicle to what I have witnessed.

RICHARD SEXTON

ACKNOWLEDGMENTS

Mural detail from the loggia of the principal house at Whitney Plantation.

I WOULD LIKE TO ACKNOWLEDGE ALL THOSE INDIVIDuals who helped make this book possible. Alex S. MacLean made the vital contribution of aerial photography. Alex is, in my opinion, the preeminent chronicler of the environment from the air, and I am honored that he was willing to make such a substantial contribution to this project. Eugene Cizek contributed the historical essay that introduces the body of the book. Cizek is one of the most noted authorities on the historic architecture of the River Road and one of the most prominent advocates for its preservation. Peter Patout, a friend and antiquarian, was my first and most enthusiastic guide to the River Road. Much of what I ultimately discovered and learned about the River Road resulted from Peter's early help and feedback. Glynne Couvillion, Norman Marmillion, Ann Wilkinson, and Earl Perry, Jr. were also helpful in providing entrée to particular plantation sites. Arthur Scully, a noted authority on the architect James Dakin, and Robert Tannen, an artist and urban planner, both generously shared their expertise with me. Dr. Jay Edwards of LSU and Barbara SoRelle Bacot of the Louisiana Department of Culture, Recreation and Tourism were both helpful in providing access to visual material used in the introduction. Martin Adamo, a former seminarian and teacher, shared his knowledge of Catholic history and tradition. Journalist Julia Reed showed great enthusiasm for this project and offered much help and feedback along the way. Marc Cooper, Director of the Vieux Carré Commission, was helpful with French translations.

I would also like to thank Jack Jensen, the publisher at Chronicle Books, who has always been receptive and supportive of my work. I'd like to thank my editors at Chronicle, Lesley Bruynesteyn and William LeBlond, who ably guided this project through to completion. I'd like to thank Vance Adams and Russ Ganser, who assisted with the photography throughout the project. I'd like to thank Charles Routhier for an outstanding book design and Pamela Geismar at Chronicle, who supervised the design effort. I'd like to thank Ann Masson, who offered very insightful feedback on my manuscript and checked it for errors. Any that remain are, of course, my own.

Finally, I'd like to thank all those individuals and institutions who allowed me to photograph their buildings and property. Without their cooperation, this book would not have been what it is. Special thanks to: Alden André, vice-president of Formosa Plastics Corporation USA (Whitney Plantation); Stacy Atkins, marketing director, Oak Alley Plantation; James J. Bailey, the Cottage Plantation ruins; Joseph E. Bourgoyne and Brenda Bourgoyne Blanchard, Marietta's Cottage; David Broussard and the parishioners of St. Gabriel Catholic Church; Michael and Claudette Davis, Desiré Plantation; Don Didier, curator, Destrehan Plantation; Richard Genre, Bocage Plantation; Douglas Hayward, Germania Plantation; Michael Hopping, Overseer's Cottage, Homestead Plantation; Teresa James, historian, and Debbie Welker, former textile curator, Nottoway Plantation; Bob and Susan Judice, L'Hermitage Plantation; Richard Keller and the owners of Home Place Plantation; A. Denis Lanaux, Glendale Plantation; Norman and Sand Marmillion, Laura Plantation; the parishioners of St. Michael's Catholic Church; Richard Naberschnig, Magnolia Lane Plantation; Bryan Pedeaux, Haydel-Jones Plantation; Jennifer Rutledge, manager, San Francisco Plantation; Matilda Gray Stream and Jane Boddie, Evergreen Plantation; Harriet Tillman and the congregation of St. John Baptist Church; Suzanne Turner, Valcour Aime Gardens; Stan J. Waguespack, Edmond Simon, Joan D. Boudreaux, and the St. Joseph P & M Corporation, Ltd., St. Joseph Plantation and Store; Noel Wheeler, external affairs manager, and Rose Martin, Shell Chemical Company (Ashland/Belle Helene Plantation); Ann Wilkinson, Poplar Grove Plantation; Leonard Zeringue, Zeringue Fruit and Vegetable Stand.

PLANTATIONS OPEN TO THE PUBLIC

SOME PLANTATION SITES FEATURED IN *VESTIGES OF Grandeur* are open to the public, as house museums or bed and breakfast accommodations or both. This list identifies the plantation houses between New Orleans and Baton Rouge currently open, whether featured within these pages or not. Any visitor to the general area should consider exploring the historical and cultural environment that exists along the River Road. The intent is for this listing to be definitive; the author apologizes for any omissions. Please note that some houses are open by appointment only. Phone numbers are given for each house. These numbers were current at the time of publication, but of course are subject to change.

Bear in mind that the philosophical concept of a house as a "museum" is diverse. Some house museums are appointed with historically correct furnishings and some are not. Some tours are mostly local lore and others are historically accurate. Some experiences are mostly entertainment; others stress education and history. Regardless, they can all be worthwhile.

Though some houses in this book are open to the public, most are not. And it is important to respect the privacy of those sites that are *not* public. The familiar marker identifying a house as a landmark does not mean that it is public. Please use this listing to identify those houses that may be visited.

DESTREHAN MANOR HOUSE
Louisiana Highway 48, east bank, in the town of Destrehan between Norco and St. Rose. Museum. 504-764-9315
This early, significant Creole house includes historically correct furnishings. Some rooms are re-creations of a particular period. For instance, a room furnished as a Freedmen's Bureau Office depicts that time after the war when the plantation became a Freedmen's Bureau.

EVERGREEN PLANTATION COMPLEX
Louisiana Highway 18, west bank, about five miles above the community of Edgard. Museum. Tours by appointment. 504-497-3837
Evergreen is the most intact plantation site on the River Road. The principal house, complemented by *garçonnières*, *pigeonniers*, a plantation office, kitchen building, and even the privy, are extant, in their

original configurations. Even one of the two slave cabin sites has survived. This site was made public in the fall of 1998 for the first time since the complex was first restored in the 1940s.

HOUMAS HOUSE
Louisiana Highway 942, east bank, near the community of Burnside. Museum. 225-473-7841

LABRANCHE PLANTATION DEPENDENCY
Louisiana Highway 48, east bank, in the town of St. Rose. Museum. 504-468-8843
The principal house no longer exists, but a rather substantial *garçonnière* remains and is the feature of the tour.

LAURA PLANTATION COMPLEX
Louisiana Highway 18, west bank, in the community of Vacherie. Museum. 225-265-7690
Laura is a relatively early house with many historical alterations. Its restoration is on-going and its richly patinated interiors are a grand evocation of the passage of time. The tour emphasizes Creole culture and is offered in both English and French.

L'HERMITAGE PLANTATION HOUSE
Louisiana Highway 942, east bank, below the community of Darrow. Open to groups by appointment only. Call for arrangements. 504-891-8493.

MAGNOLIA MOUND PLANTATION HOUSE
Nicholson Drive, Baton Rouge. Museum. 225-343-4955

MARIETTA'S COTTAGE AND MISS LOUISA'S HOUSE
Nadler Street, off Louisiana Highway 1, in the Old Turnerville District of Plaquemine. Museum. 225-687-5337 or 225-687-6029.
These houses, which face each other on Nadler Street, are not plantation houses but are modest, small-town, nineteenth-century cottages.

NOTTOWAY PLANTATION HOUSE
Louisiana Highway 1, west bank, near White Castle. Museum. Bed and Breakfast. Restaurant. 225-545-2730
Nottoway is the largest antebellum house surviving on the River Road.

OAK ALLEY PLANTATION HOUSE
Louisiana Highway 18, west bank, between the communities of Vacherie and St. James. Museum. Bed and Breakfast. Restaurant. 225-265-2151
The impressive *allée* of twenty-eight live oaks, planted in the early eighteenth century, is unprecedented on the River Road.

ORMOND PLANTATION HOUSE
Louisiana Highway 48, east bank, near Destrehan. Museum. 504-764-8544

POPLAR GROVE PLANTATION HOUSE
North River Road, west bank, Port Allen. Museum. Tours by appointment. 225-344-3913

SAN FRANCISCO PLANTATION HOUSE
Louisiana Highway 44, east bank, near Garyville. Museum. 504-535-2341

TEZCUCO PLANTATION HOUSE
Louisiana Highway 44, east bank, below the community of Burnside. Museum. Bed and Breakfast. 225-562-3929
In addition to the house museum, this site features the Museum of African-American History. Tours of the African-American museum are by appointment only. 225-644-7955, for arrangements.

GLOSSARY

Detail of a masonry Tuscan column at Whitney Plantation.

Acadian *(Cajun, coll.)*: The people of French ancestry who were exiled from their colonial homeland, Acadia—now know as Nova Scotia—by the British after the fall of French Canada, and their associated culture. The Acadians gradually resettled themselves in Louisiana, where they found cultural acceptance and flourished.

allée (sometimes called alley): Paired lines of planted trees forming an arcade, and typically framing a view, between the principal house of a plantation and the river.

Anglo: Of or pertaining to English culture and its derivative cultures, namely American. Historically, the Creoles used the term American instead of Anglo.

antebellum: The period immediately preceding the American Civil War romantically portrayed as the American South's halcyon era. The reciprocal term, postbellum, refers to that period after the war or after Reconstruction.

arpent: An archaic linear unit of French measure approximately equal to 192 American feet. French colonial land grants were measured in arpents. Square arpents, equal to about 5/6ths of an acre, were sometimes used.

batture *(bacher)*: That area of land on the river side of the levee, unprotected from flooding, that could be commercially developed, as a port or docking facility, for instance.

bousillage (boo-see-yaj: sometimes called mud-and-moss): A construction method where the wall spaces between wooden heavy-timber framing members were infilled with river mud held together with Spanish moss or animal hair spread over a lath made of sticks.

brick-between-post *(briquette entre poteaux):* A construction method where the wall spaces between wooden heavy-timber framing members were infilled with bricks and mortar.

cabinet (ca-bin-ay): A small room, typically one of a pair, at the rear of a Creole house plan flanking an open porch or loggia. A *cabinet* typically served as storage, or some other utilitarian purpose, such as a bathing room.

classical: In common architectural use, inspired by or derived from the temple forms and detailing of ancient Greek and Roman architecture. This term incorporates the classically derived Federal and Greek Revival styles.

colombage (co-lum-baj): The French term for heavy timber framing.

Creole: The people born in the New World of European—predominantly French or Spanish—descent, and their associated culture. A Creole of color is a person of mixed race—European and African or Native American or some combination of both.

Creole cottage: A squarish house plan consisting of four adjoining main rooms laid out symmetrically without hallways between. A Creole cottage is side-gabled with a pitched roof, sometimes incorporating one or two dormers in the roof slopes. At the rear of the house is a loggia flanked by *cabinet.* The Creole cottage is a smaller urban derivative of the Creole plantation house plan.

Federal: A classically derived style of American architecture following and related to Georgian. It is sometimes referred to as Adam or Adamesque, after the Adam brothers, British architects who were the major proponents of the style. In the U. S., the Federal style was prominent from about 1780 to 1820.

French colonial: In architectural use, of or pertaining to the method of building utilized by the French in their New World colonies. In Louisiana, the French colonial period technically ended in 1763, but persisted through natural cultural predilections under the Spanish and into the early American periods. As late as the 1830s and 1840s, new plantation architecture in Louisiana was constructed with French colonial influences.

gallery: Derived from the French *galerie,* referring to an architectural space adjoining an interior room, open to the outdoors and covered by a roof overhang; synonymous with porch.

garçonnière: Literally, French for "boy's place." A separate residential quarter that in its most literal form was intended as transitional housing for the male children of the household approaching adulthood. In practice, *garçonnières* were used for a variety of purposes and were the equivalent of outbuildings or guest cottages.

German Coast (*Côte des Allemands*): An area of the River Road near the present day community of Hahnville, on the west bank, where Swiss and German peasants, many of them from Alsace-Lorraine, were given land grants by the French. Initially, German Coast residents operated small farms and raised livestock, which helped sustain the urban population of New Orleans.

Greek key: A method of detailing the trim around a door or window that emulates post and lintel construction of the temples of ancient Greece. The Greek key is a distinguishing characteristic of Greek Revival architecture.

Greek Revival: A style of architecture derived from the temple forms of ancient Greece. In the U. S., the Greek Revival was popular from about 1820 to the Civil War. It was the dominant style of the antebellum architecture of the American South.

levee: A term derived from French meaning to "raise up," that describes the dike or embankment built to contain the annual spring flood of the river. Originally, each plantation owner or land grant recipient was required to erect and maintain a levee at their property's river frontage. After the Great Flood in 1927, the federal government and the U. S. Army Corps of Engineers took control of the levee system.

parterre garden: A formal garden plan, derived from the French, consisting of trimmed hedges planted in a regimented axial pattern, creating borders for pathways and for beds infilled with a variety of plantings. Creole plantations typically incorporated parterre gardens at the rear of the principal house and were used as a landscaping element uniting outbuildings.

perique tobacco: A variety of pungent tobacco cultivated on the River Road whose primary use was in cigar making, where it was typically blended with milder tobaccos to impart a distinctive flavor.

pieux fencing: A fence of rough-hewn, pointed cypress planks stuck into the ground and joined together by horizontal cross members. *Pieux* fences enclosed the principal house and outbuildings on Creole plantations. They were derived from the palisades surrounding early French colonial forts, such as Fort Maurepas built in 1699.

pigeonnier: A cote for pigeons or squab, which were raised on Creole plantations as a food source and for their guano, which was used as fertilizer. *Pigeonniers* were a significant decorative element complementing the garden and principal house of the plantation and were typically sited in pairs, one on each side of the principal house.

plantation: A major agricultural concern established for the purpose of producing a crop to be sold for profit at market.

sugarhouse: A processing facility on a plantation where cane juice is extracted from the stalk, clarified, and then crystallized into raw sugar. Synonymous with sugar mill but not with sugar refinery, which converts raw sugar into refined white sugar.

BIBLIOGRAPHY

Delehanty, Randolph. *Art in the American South: Works from the Ogden Collection.* Baton Rouge: Louisiana State University Press, 1996.

Gleason, David King. *Plantation Homes of Louisiana and the Natchez Area.* Baton Rouge: Louisiana State University Press, 1982.

Gross, Steve, Susan Daley, and Henry Wiencek. *Old Houses.* New York: Stewart, Tabori & Chang, 1991.

Guidry, Emily Chenet. *Bonfires on the Levee.* St. James Parish: St. James Parish Historical Society, 1994.

Kane, Harnett T. *Plantation Parade: The Grand Manner in Louisiana.* New York: William Morrow & Co., 1945.

Kennedy, Roger G. *Greek Revival America.* New York: Stewart, Tabori & Chang, 1989.

Lane, Mills. *Architecture of the Old South: Louisiana.* New York: Beehive Press, 1990.

Laughlin, Clarence John. *Ghosts along the Mississippi: The Magic of the Old Houses of Louisiana.* New York: Charles Scribner and Sons, 1948.

McAlester, Virginia and Lee McAlester. *A Field Guide to American Houses.* New York: Alfred A Knopf, 1984.

Poesch, Jessie, and Barbara Bacot, eds. *Louisiana Buildings 1720–1940: The Historic American Buildings Survey.* Baton Rouge: Louisiana State University Press, 1997.

Saxon, Lyle. *Gumbo Ya-Ya: Folk Tales of Louisiana.* Baton Rouge: Louisiana Library Commission, 1945.

Saxon, Lyle. *New Orleans City Guide. Federal Writers Project of the WPA.* Boston: Houghton-Mifflin Co., 1938.

Scully, Vincent. *American Architecture and Urbanism,* rev. ed. New York: Henry Holt, 1988.

Sternberg, Mary Ann. *Along the River Road: Past and Present on Louisiana's Historic Byway.* Baton Rouge: Louisiana State University Press, 1996.

INDEX

ABOUT THE AUTHOR
AND CONTRIBUTORS

The plantation bell from Uncle Sam Plantation. This is the only known vestige from Uncle Sam, one of the most elaborate, classically detailed plantation complexes on the River Road.

RICHARD SEXTON was born in Atlanta and was raised in Colquitt, a small farming town in southwest Georgia. He is a noted photographer, writer, and speaker on the topics of architecture and the built environment. Sexton is the author-photographer of *The Cottage Book* and *Parallel Utopias: The Quest for Community,* and coauthor/photographer of the best-selling *New Orleans: Elegance and Decadence* and *In the Victorian Style,* all from Chronicle Books. He has produced features for such publications as *Abitare,* the *San Francisco Examiner's Image Magazine, Northern California Home & Garden,* and *Preservation in Print.* His photographs have appeared in the *Los Angeles Times Magazine, Louisiana Life, New Orleans Magazine,* the *New York Times, Preservation,* and *Smithsonian,* among others. He speaks frequently at events such as the Planning Conference of the American Institute of Architects and the National Design Conference of the American Institute of Graphic Arts. Since 1991, he has resided in New Orleans where he lives in an 1834 Creole townhouse in the French Quarter.

ALEX S. MACLEAN founded Landslides, a Boston-based aerial photography firm, in 1975. His aerial images provide a vital perspective on the realtionship between the natural and constructed environments. MacLean is the author/photographer of the book *Look at the Land,* and coauthor/photographer of *Taking Measures across the American Landscape.* He lives in the Boston area.

EUGENE CIZEK, PH.D., FAIA, is an architect who has supervised the restoration of many Louisiana landmarks, including such River Road plantations as Destrehan and Laura. Director of the Historic American Buildings Survey for the Bayou-River Road, he has been a professor of architecture at Tulane University since 1970 and is the cofounder/director of Tulane's Education through Historic Preservation program. Cizek is a Fellow of the American Institute of Architects and a frequent writer on the topic of historic architecture and its preservation. He lives in the Faubourg Marigny neighborhood of New Orleans.

V